COLIN GRANT

Colin Grant is an author, historian and critic. He has written acclaimed biographies of the Wailers and of Marcus Garvey. *Bageye at the Wheel*, his memoir of growing up in a Caribbean family in 1970s Luton, was shortlisted for the PEN Ackerley Prize. His history of epilepsy, *A Smell of Burning*, was a *Sunday Times* Book of the Year. His book *Homecoming: Voices of the Windrush Generation* was a BBC Radio 4 Book of the Week and *Daily Telegraph* Book of the Year. He is director of WritersMosaic and a fellow of the Royal Society of Literature.

ALSO BY COLIN GRANT

COLIN GRANT

I'm Black So You Don't Have to Be

A memoir in eight lives

VINTAGE

1 3 5 7 9 10 8 6 4 2

Vintage is part of the Penguin Random House group of companies
whose addresses can be found at global.penguinrandomhouse.com

First published in Vintage in 2024
First published in hardback by Jonathan Cape in 2023

'The Recall of Herman Harcourt' was first published in
Granta 140: State of Mind, Summer 2017.

penguin.co.uk/vintage

Printed and bound in Great Britain by Clays Ltd, Elcograf S.p.A.

The authorised representative in the EEA is Penguin Random House Ireland,
Morrison Chambers, 32 Nassau Street, Dublin D02 YH68

A CIP catalogue record for this book is available from the British Library

ISBN 9781529918366

Penguin Random House is committed to a sustainable future
for our business, our readers and our planet. This book is made
from Forest Stewardship Council® certified paper.

To Ethlyn

Contents

Preface

'When was the last time you gave the nod?' a black friend asked me recently.

'The black nod?'

'What other nod is there?' he answered.

I was delighted by the question.

'You know!' I chuckled at the memory of it, and the sudden sweep of nostalgia.

My friend joined in. 'That's what I'm talking about!'

We were talking about that subtle and secret signal one black person would give whenever they saw another on any British street in my youth. The black nod said, 'I see you' at a time in this country when, let's face it, you were mostly invisible; that is, until you were unfortunate enough to – uh oh, here we go – attract the attention of white people who suddenly realised you were not like them. Back in the day, the black nod was like those moments in the Second World War films we loved, when nervous British escapees from German prisoner-of-war camps, with not a lick of the German language between them, passed each other on the streets of Berlin in dread of being discovered.

In Luton, where I grew up the son of Jamaican parents, you could counter that threat of discovery if you paid attention to your parents' warning: 'play fool fi ketch wise'. The Caribbean proverb was a code and instruction to mask your feelings, to be knowingly humble so that you weren't thought of by 'the man' as an enemy combatant and could get along in British life unmolested. The saying, 'play fool fi ketch wise' originated in the days of slavery as a strategy for avoiding massa's wrath and the driver's whip. But it still seemed sensible to practise it throughout my childhood and early adulthood in the 1970s and 80s.

Not revealing too much of myself has served me well as a writer. But it has also made my subject, the study of Caribbean people in Britain, a challenge, because playing fool fi ketch wise is also a very Caribbean obfuscation, and the reality that you're trying to capture seems forever beyond your grasp. Yet there's a kind of frequency, a magical one, that my antennae have tuned to in the company of Jamaicans who've voyaged alongside me over the decades. They're really the subjects of this memoir but, if you read carefully, you'll find me reflected in the eight true stories that form the core of this book.

In family constellation therapy, a volunteer replaces you: let's call her A. She's your proxy. A stands in the middle of a circle surrounded by other volunteers who act as proxies for your family members. Given prompts and directions, the stand-ins then articulate scenes from your life. Positioned outside of the circle, you observe A and the other characters playing your family, and in doing so, you might gain fresh insights into your family dynamic.

In a way, that's how this book unfolds. It's always tempting to cast yourself as the hero in a memoir, but you can't sustain that fiction when your characters start leaking truths about you. In the unguarded detail of the stories, the influence of these people on my nature and identity becomes clearer. My mentoring uncle, Castus, we both agreed, was smarter than me, but had not been granted any of the opportunities offered to me. I sailed through life easily because my uncle, who arrived in Britain from Jamaica in the year I was born, had endured a gauntlet of prejudice on my behalf, being racialised by a country that only saw his blackness. 'I'm black,' he'd say to me, 'so you don't have to be.'

The characters in the book are real-life ones. I've disguised some of the names; not to spare blushes, but because Jamaicans are the most litigious people on the planet. They're characters because they're approximations. But, though grounded in reality, they shuttle between fiction and fact – in the Jamaican sense: Jamaicans contend that there are no facts, only versions.

I've generally read non-fiction to find out about facts; I read fiction to see truths about myself through the rich tapestry of fictionalised lives, as if in a metaphorical tailor shop, trying on bespoke personalities and characteristics. Though this memoir is non-fiction, you may see aspects of yourself reflected here, too.

When I was younger, I was always terrified of people finding out what I really felt, which is a bit of a problem when, decades later, you write a book with the intention of being revelatory. Wouldn't it be daring and a relief, I thought, to be able to write with the same candour with which I express myself in the safety and company of close friends and relations? Finally, I settled on the idea that in writing *I'm Black So You Don't Have to Be*, I was giving the reader the black nod.

Doc Saunders

Carry go, bring come

All families have a hierarchy. In our family there were several tiers, but the bottom rung was reserved permanently for my grand-uncle, Doc Saunders. Relatives were often critical of him. He was said to have told 'too many lie' and was 'too white-minded' in his fawning preference for white people. Most damningly, he'd been assailed for selling, without consulting anyone, Aunt Anita's prized violin that she'd once played at Carnegie Hall and had left in his care before she died.

No one had spoken to Doc Saunders in over a decade, but when I was nineteen and was offered a place as a medical student at The London Hospital, he appeared to be a possible saviour. The school was based in Whitechapel: an area our family knew very little about, other than it was a bad square to land on in Monopoly. Arriving there in 1981, the Monopoly board didn't seem to be wrong. Whitechapel felt neglected, riddled with clapboard houses whose walls would wobble if you brushed too heavily alongside them; condemned buildings lined every other street, boarded-up, disfigured by corrugated-iron barricades and rusting barbed wire. The prospect of living there was not enticing.

All the rooms in the student halls of residence had gone, and I hadn't yet made any friends among the privileged bohemians who clubbed together to rent houses in slightly less seedy neighbourhoods, like Bethnal Green. After a week of commuting from my hometown, Luton, it was clear I'd have to find somewhere in London. That's when Doc Saunders's name first came up.

He was a sweet-back, a saga boy, a man who'd made never-ending courtships his life's work. This is what I knew: he was a pioneer, arriving in Britain before World War II, and had thoroughly enjoyed himself, before tens of thousands of other West Indians showed up to spoil the party. Overnight, he'd gone from being an exotic curiosity to just another irksome darky. But even as the competition mounted, this red-meat-eating, glistening toreador of a man, around whom no one in a blouse-n-skirt was safe, had continued to attract a string of women, happy to act as warming pans in between the sheets, so long as Doc Saunders, whatever games he played, came home to them.

Those are the facts. But how anyone knew these facts was a mystery, because Doc Saunders hadn't exchanged two words with any member of our extended family since the war began; not the World War but the family war, which in our family was much the same.

The war began when Doc Saunders came ashore in the late 1930s, and 'sold' that violin – long-cherished by the extended family – to a stranger, the first white man who had a few kind words to say to him, so the story went.

Given the glamour attached to his name in the family, I assumed Doc Saunders would have practised on Harley Street and lived fashionably in Belgravia. He did not. For the last thirty years, he'd been confined to somewhere called Manor House. Never mind Whitechapel, Manor House didn't even feature on the Monopoly board. At a family conference, it had been decided that Doc Saunders could be shamed into putting me up temporarily in his flat, until something better came up.

He was in his eighties, had never married and lived alone;

he'd consciously cut himself off from the rest of us. But most of the family agreed that this was a chance for the old reprobate to redeem himself. And besides, he ought to welcome the company. Their logic was compelling and simple: Doc Saunders and I would be 'two doctors under one roof'.

I'd never met my grand-uncle, but as a child I'd imagined a man in a long grey coat down to his ankles; a close fit for the consumptive, gun-slinging 'Doc Holliday' in the Westerns. Of all the fellas who came round our house, I reckoned Joe Barnes (who was almost family) would know better; so I went looking for Joe. If you wanted the unvarnished truth, Joe was your man. He was known for always greeting the fellas with an insult. Most of the men were 'ugly jackasses' or, if he was feeling generous, just 'ugly', or just 'jackasses'. Joe would breeze into a room, lay eyes on one of the ugly jackasses and complain loudly: 'Rass, my day spoil already.'

He'd always been the one adult who'd descend to our level to talk to us as kids. Even now, I think of him on one knee. But when I asked Joe what Doc Saunders was really like, he did something I'd never seen before: he paused. I could see his mind racing through various permutations; pulling out drawers of thought before slamming them shut.

'Why you ask?' said Joe, finally.

'I'm supposed to go live with him.'

'Rass, for how long?'

'Not sure. Just a cotch, till I find somewhere.'

'You don't have no other choice?' asked Joe.

I shook my head.

'Well, I might say, it could be worse. But I don't like tell no lie.'

Joe wouldn't be drawn further, except to say: 'Ask him wha'appen to the violin.'

*

5

Although I'd written down careful instructions, I had not allowed for the possibility of more than one exit from the Underground station, each as bewildering as the other. I was lost immediately in the unforgiving streets of Manor House. It wouldn't create a great first impression, but I surrendered to the idea that I'd have to call the flat. I made my way to a phone box. A tall youth with a prominent Afro, and wearing a long sheepskin coat, was propped up inside like a half-opened flick knife. His head leaned on the window pane. He was not on the phone but obviously had no intention of vacating the box. He gave me one of those discouraging looks – the 'I'm going to be in here just as long as I damn well please' variety. The phone rang. He picked up and replaced the receiver straight away. Seconds later, it rang again. This time he picked it up, held it at arm's length and slowly brought it to his ear.

'Stop your noise! Listen,' he said. 'Listen, listen, listen!' Each 'listen' was louder than the previous one. 'No, no. Listen!' He slammed down the receiver and took a second before picking it up again. He caught my eye as he dialled a number and pushed a coin into the slot. But he didn't speak into the phone. He popped his head out the door. 'Boss, boss. Do me a favour.' He held out the phone to me. 'Can you talk to her?'

I was dismayed.

'C'mon, man. She's doing my head in. She's just not listening. But she'll listen to you.'

I should have just walked away, but he was insistent. I took the phone. The woman let loose a stream of obscenities. When I tried to speak, she paused.

'Who's is this? Digs?'

'Tell her I check by she later,' whispered Digs.

'He prefers to defer your meeting till later.'

'What?'

The pips started going on the phone but when I looked to Digs, he just shrugged. I slid out a coin from my trouser pocket and slotted it into the machine. The woman continued to scream and commanded me to take down her number in case Digs had forgotten it.

'You got a pen?'

I fumbled inside my jacket for a pen, but Digs waved for the phone.

'I'm putting Digs back on,' I said.

He shooed me out of the booth, and closed the door, wedging it shut with his foot. He cackled loudly down the phone. I could hear his girlfriend laughing as well. There was another phone box about a hundred yards down the road and I phoned Doc Saunders's number. A mature-sounding woman answered, and she unnerved me by describing exactly what I was wearing. 'You're right outside,' she said. 'Come to the third floor.'

The flat was in a block once entirely run by the council – solid, brick-built and plain. A handful of tenants had taken up the new offer of right-to-buy. You could tell them by their very first act of ownership: replacing front doors with modern plasticised versions and matching flower pots, in contrast to the standard racing-green wooden doors of the council stock. Doc Saunders was in the latter camp. I thought it peculiar that a doctor would be living here, especially one who inspired such rancour and envy among his relatives.

The same woman who I presumed answered the phone also answered the front door. She was more elderly than I expected. Her thin lips were painted and the blush was a little overdone on her cheeks. I'd have scrutinised her more if I hadn't been distracted by the transparent plastic gloves that she wore.

'I was just leaving.'

She sounded like it had been agreed in advance, perhaps

because of my arrival. 'I'm Mrs McBride, but you can call me Betty,' she said with a jauntiness that belied her business-like manner. Betty directed me instantly to my bedroom. It was stark and monastic, but quite appealing really, especially as I'd never had my own room. Once I'd put down my bag, I should have wandered out and introduced myself, but I could hear Betty and my grand-uncle whispering. Some unspecified sense of shame trapped me in that room for so long that my non-appearance risked attracting attention. I counted to ten before leaving.

Doc Saunders sat with his back to me in the living room with a large bath towel draped across his shoulders.

'How you like the room?' He spoke in a rich, salty voice, laced with irony. 'If you expecting grandeur, you come too soon.' His laughter turned into a coughing fit. He was still coughing when Betty, removing her gloves, pulled the ends of the towel up and over his head and patted and rubbed his hair dry before running a comb through it. Her treatment of the old man was something more than professional. There was tenderness in the way she left her hands on his shoulders afterwards, until his hands reached back to join hers. A minute passed like that with them in silent communion before she began gathering the kit and the rest of her things from around the flat.

Walking was not easy for her. Betty's hips were stiff. I imagined them fused. She moved briskly, leaning forward, setting off with the tiny staccato steps of a year-old child learning to walk, speeding up on reaching safety at the end of the perilous trial run. She opened and closed the front door behind her without so much as a goodbye.

It didn't seem right to call him Doc Saunders. He wasn't too fond of 'great-' or 'grand-uncle'. He insisted I just call him Percy. I asked him about Betty and he simply answered 'lady friend', in a way that did not invite further questions.

I'd heard the rumours, of course. Doc Saunders was scorned, but also pitied as one of those foolish black men whose head was turned; who was flattered by the company of whites. Pitied because such men were fooled into thinking that their association with English women distinguished them, when really everyone understood that if a white woman went with a black man, then it was safe to assume she'd go with any black man.

No one really knew the extent of Doc Saunders's delusion because of the decades-long breach from the family, during which he'd even gone to the length of changing his name from Algon Adams to Percival Saunders. There was some grumbling about what lessons I might learn from such a nasty old man who frequented blue foots. If I hadn't needed somewhere to stay, the family would have left him to stew in his own juices.

Such men ('You see how black man chupid,' my mum had often argued) couldn't be trusted. The old-timers recalled with disgust how Garfield Sobers had 'sell out, marry white!' and how badly he performed in test matches playing for the West Indies once he'd married an Australian woman (a marginal improvement on if she'd been English).

I steered the conversation onto safer ground, to Doc Saunders's career, and asked him what he specialised in, but he looked confused.

'What branch of medicine, I mean?'

Percy let rip a sad little laugh.

'You are a doctor?'

'Nope.'

If that was the case, I asked him, then why did everyone call him Doc Saunders?

He said, a little sourly, that it was because he used to drive ambulances.

'I heard you were a doctor.'

9

'You heard wrong.'

'But didn't you study medicine?'

'It look like I study medicine? You see any patient line up outside the door?'

'I assumed you were retired.'

'Bwoi, keep this up, I soon retire you.'

Percy let the threat hang in the air and went off to check on a pot on the stove. Cupboard doors were opened and slammed shut. Cutlery was roughly removed from a drawer. But by the time he returned, he must have decided to take pity on the village idiot he'd allowed into his home because he said with a smile: 'I'm retired now. Haven't drive an ambulance in a long time.'

'But they say I take after you,' I said, 'that we already have one doctor in the family. Now we'll have two. They've been saying it ever since.'

'Ever since?'

'Since time,' I answered.

'Oh, so you can talk like a countryman?'

'When I ready,' I said in the thickest, richest patois I could manage.

Percy laughed so hard his chest rocked. He sat down to compose himself and took a cigarette from a packet. He did so hesitantly, like a man who'd promised to cut down and had forgotten whether he'd already exceeded his quota for the day. It was hard not to stare at his hands as Uncle Percy lit up, because he wore a pair of lightweight, white cotton gloves. I had a flash of remembrance of people mentioning he'd also been a fire warden during the War. Perhaps the gloves had something to do with that.

'Not many black doctors,' said Percy. 'You must be a pioneer. Plenty coolie, but not much black. As a matter of fact, from I come here, I only run across one black doctor, and he wasn't all that black. Haircut. One smart black man.'

'Why'd they call him Haircut?'

'Don't be idiot,' said Percy. 'The haircut business almost bankrupt him.'

'That's a funny name. What was his real name?'

'Me just done tell you him name.'

'Yes, but what was his real name?' I asked.

Percy let out a long, weary-sounding 'Bwoiiiii.' He shook his head: 'How long you plan stay in my yard?'

I'd been warned that Doc Saunders could be 'funny' with people. But I'd never considered until this moment how unenthusiastic he might have been about me coming to stay; how he might have given in reluctantly to the relatives. He lit another cigarette. Nothing accused or forgave as quickly and unequivocally as a cigarette. He inhaled the familiar hope and exhaled the bad vibes, which had lingered in the air since Betty's departure. 'Me and you will get on better if you don't ask so many question.'

I wasn't to ask about the lipstick and compact on the windowsill of the bathroom, or the open birdcage, or the pair of finches who flew freely around the flat. I was not to suggest opening the windows to release the cigarette smoke (smoke was preferable to cold air), or to inquire about how the war with the Adams family began and when or if it would ever end. Anything about the white gloves obviously would not be entertained. If I managed all these things, then he and I would have no argument; we'd get on just fine.

The next morning, as I prepared to leave, Percy called me back from the front door.

'Where you going like that?'

'Just off to college.'

'Like that? You gwan leave my yard like that? Like a ragamuffin?'

I looked down at my new shirt and trousers with an exemplary crease.

'Stop puke around. Suppose anyone did see?'

I was commanded to go and fetch a tie from the wardrobe in his bedroom, and he watched and nodded approvingly as I fashioned a Windsor knot. Each subsequent departure for medical school began the same way – with the kind of inspection I'd last endured from my mother as a child. After that first morning, I always allowed myself a little extra time, even though I never had any trouble waking up at Percy's.

With time – and I was to stay there months longer than either of us had imagined – I grew fond of Percy. I told him that with his pencil-thin moustache and Hollywood-matinee good looks, he reminded me of Errol Flynn. 'Douglas Fairbanks Junior,' he corrected.

Percy had that Adams trait of exaggeration that was both amusing and vexing, erudite and coarse. Did I have a girlfriend, he wanted to know, or any 'pum pum', as he put it, ploughing on in the absence of a response from me.

'Black or white? I hope she white. I done with black women. Me not want none of them, and none of them pickney neither. This world nah need no more Adams. Damn West Indians take up too much room, make too much noise. When people ask where I from, I say I from South America. What do I do? I'm something in the City. After that, they don't ask again.'

I forgave him his verbal jousting; my father, Bageye, had also been like that with his spars. It was a West Indian thing, and even though Percy was harsher than most, I attempted to laugh along with him. I was so keen to meet his approval that I sometimes imagined I was auditioning to be his son – the son, he said, he never had.

Each morning, from Percy's bedroom, I'd hear feeble attempts to clear his throat; then a round of violent coughing, followed by a strange rumbling across his chest, a wet snapping, bubbling sound, like a pan of water on the boil. Through an extraordinary feat of rationality, Percy had concluded that the coughing spasms could only be relieved by a cigarette. Finishing off that first ciggie, on the way to the toilet he rattled on my door: 'Hands off cocks. On with socks.' It was his longest-serving joke. Afterwards, he'd proceed to release the finches. 'I can't bear to see them locked up,' he'd announce, all watery eyed. It never seemed to occur to him that the limits of his flat were only a marginal improvement on the birdcage: it was still a cage, only bigger. The sight of the birds encouraged to perch on Percy's cereal bowl and share his breakfast was enough to put me off my cornflakes.

His tenderness towards the finches was not extended to me. Percy was the most consistently cantankerous man I'd ever met. He made Bageye and even Monty (the most notorious of Bageye's gambling spars) seem sweet, and Monty was so mean with money and generally 'bad-minded' it was said he must have been boiled in brine.

When he berated me, though, I had the feeling he was actually berating someone else. It was the same as when Bageye argued with my mother. Bageye was really arguing with his father and his father before him, all the way back to the forebear from Africa robbed of his agency who, when the time came, submitted to enslavement and didn't kill himself; the man whose misfortune had led us here. It was never going to be pretty.

So yes, when Percy chastised me, I stood in for someone

who shadowed his life. Even aged nineteen, I could see his brusque manner was the bluff of a ruined man who long ago had departed from a more noble idea of himself, an idea that had been complicated by the arrival, perhaps, of more able West Indians – ones who weren't seeing out what little life they'd left in a council flat in Manor House. My youth and expected rewards of a future medical career must have been unbearable for him.

If I listened carefully at night when he felt sure that I'd fallen asleep, sometimes even before, another kind of personality revealed itself – a more playful one. Then, through some weird role reversal, I became the old fuddy-duddy who retired early to bed with his cup of hot chocolate whilst Percy tiptoed round the living room with Betty like adolescent lovers bent on mischief.

Their relationship was built on cigarettes: she rationed his intake. At the end of an evening, she'd withdraw a handful of cigarettes. After much faux whining and protracted outrage, Percy would capitulate. As soon as the cigarette monitor had left, he'd open the trunk where several cartons of Superkings were stashed and replace the missing handful. More often than maybe he realised, when he'd overdone it – with the tar and smoke exacerbating his undiagnosed emphysema – Betty would be summoned back to the flat to calm him down, to hold his hand and keep a watchful eye overnight in case his condition worsened.

I always thought it strange that they kept up the pretence of a bed being made up on the sofa for Betty to stop over, even though I was likely to get up in the night to discover the living room empty and the blankets and sheets unruffled. I'd have no choice but to rise early because it was too disturbing to lie there, trying not to focus on the noises coming from Percy and

Betty in the bedroom next door. The morning after those nights, I was sure to be out of the flat before they surfaced.

Digs, too, must also have been an early riser. Every day on the way to the Underground, I passed him. He always wore the same ill-fitting and slightly tatty, heavy sheepskin coat. It wasn't that he was homeless – he didn't give off that vibe – but it was bizarre that he was always there. I'd begun to wonder whether there was a way of avoiding the phone box; whether there was an alternative route from Doc Saunders's flat to the Tube station that didn't involve passing by Digs in the booth, either on the phone or waiting for it to ring. If not, then I was bound to at least nod at him. We hadn't yet reached the stage in 1981 where a black man could pass another without acknowledgement, without the black man's salute.

Each time I approached, if Digs was on the phone, he'd crack open the door, hold the receiver out for me and whisper: 'Work some magic for me, nah bredren.' Time and again, I declined, until one day he stopped asking. He recognised that the joke had run its course.

I found out his name.

'Virgil?'

'Yep.'

'Virgil,' I said. 'As in F.A.B., Virgil?'

'All systems are go,' he replied. It was a line from the kids' show *Thunderbirds*, and I was glad to be reminded of it, and that we had it in common. Thereafter, we developed a little routine. As I approached the phone booth, he'd stick his head out the door and ask, 'All systems are go?' And I'd reply, 'F.A.B., Virgil.'

We went on like this for several weeks and then one day I passed by, and he looked up but barely acknowledged me. The second time it happened, I stopped and said, 'F.A.B., Virgil?' But he wasn't in the mood.

'How's work going?' I asked, for the want of something better to say.

'Nah, nah, nah, nah, no.' Virgil gave it some thought: 'I haven't worked for the past . . .' He checked himself and brightening said confidently, 'I haven't worked for the past. I'm working towards the future.' But then he had a sudden idea. He was feeling a little nervous about an opening he wanted to check up on. Would I dial it and screen the call? If the person who answered sounded friendly, I'd pass the phone to him. It didn't make a lot of sense, but I agreed to it. Virgil shouted out the number as I dialled. Halfway through, I had a vague feeling of recognition. The phone rang. Betty answered. I slammed down the phone so hard that Virgil winced and blinked involuntarily.

I made to leave the booth. The door was open, but Virgil leaned back on it with his foot up on the doorframe, blocking my path. He jutted out his jaw the way some older women did when checking in a mirror for wrinkles on their necks.

'How long have we known each other?' asked Virgil, 'A couple of months? I guess we've missed a few stages in our relationship – is that fair?'

I said I knew what he meant; that we weren't really friends, not yet, but we were more than acquaintances.

'Exactly!' said Virgil. 'Not friends as such, 'cause friendship must be earned. Do you agree? If I make a friend, it's like swans. It's for life. You get me? A friend calls me?' At this point, Virgil slapped one hand hard with the other. 'Bang! I'm there. I got your back.' He made a pretend phone out of his hand, pushing his thumb into his ear and little finger over his mouth. 'What you need? Need something? You, my friend, you can ask me anything. Any likkle t'ing!'

I was aware of his rising agitation as he spoke.

'Go on, then. Ask me something,' he said.

There were lots of questions. Of course there were. But I couldn't voice them. Not now.

'OK, what? Nothing? Nada?' He asked. 'You got nothing for me? Let's even it up. As we're spars, I'd just like to know, if it's not too much trouble . . .' He leaned forward until I could feel the heat from his breath on my ear, and whispered: 'What the fuck is your game – with Percy?' He pulled back to give himself more room to shout: 'I mean. What! The! Fuck?'

Later that evening, I began to recount the event after dinner with Betty and Uncle Percy, but soon dried up when I sensed Percy bristle. I was interfering with his routine. Once the plates had been washed and cleared away, it was the allotted time for the word search. There were a dozen or so searches in each little booklet, and the evening couldn't come to an end until the last search had been completed. Then he'd slap down the defeated pamphlet on the table with a satisfactory sigh, and announce: 'You know what my doctor tell me? "Mr Saunders, you have the brain of a sixty-year-old man!"' I did know because eighty-something-year-old Uncle Percy was so fond of the sentiment that he was known to repeat it. 'Sixty, you know? Sixty!' Occasionally though, as now, the patterns refused to reveal their truths to the word-search wizard: they were beyond him.

'To hell with it, man,' he raged.

'Really, I don't know why you get so worked up about it,' said Betty.

Despite her soothing tone, Percy became increasingly irritated by his inability to crack the code.

'But, but this don' make sense.'

'Maybe it's a printing error?' suggested Betty.

'Nah must,' Percy answered. 'Pure printing error in the t'ing.'

His pen ranged violently over the page, dismissing the internal logic of the search in favour of his own idiosyncratic, but pleasing groupings of letters that bore little correlation to actual words. He showed the final result to Betty and she nodded. It was close enough.

Restored to a better mood and prompted now by his lady friend, Percy asked me to go back over what I'd been saying. We often seemed to have trouble maintaining the thread of a conversation, but this time it was easier. Percy chortled – not so loudly that it could be misconstrued as encouragement, but enough for me to keep going. Soon though, the chuckling trailed off, and Percy began to ask for more details. He demanded to know how far away the phone box was, and what the stranger looked like. As Virgil had taken up camp in a phone box just a few hundred yards away, I was surprised by Percy's claim that he'd never noticed him. Percy's ire seemed to peak when I let slip that Virgil was black. I say 'black': he was fairer skinned than me, yet he was blacker, appeared undiluted black, in ways that I could only dream of being.

'How black?' Percy tapped the edge of the wooden table. 'Blacker than this?'

'Cinnamon-coloured, I'd say. If you really are asking,' I said. 'Cinnamon – like the spice. You know, coffee-coloured. I think one of his parents may be on the white side.'

Percy shot out of his seat. 'Yes Lord,' he wailed. 'You see the hand of the devil?' I'd never seen him so visibly discomfited. He wheezed and coughed into a handkerchief.

'This cinnamon – he never give you anything bring come?' said Percy. 'You sure? Check your pockets? Go check.' There was nothing in my coat pocket, but I judged it wise to humour him and go to the hallway and take a look. All the while, Percy was complaining. Betty encouraged him to keep his voice down, but he didn't care that I heard. He wanted me to hear that he knew it was a set-up – that I'd been sent.

'Is she send him here – Satan!'

By 'she', he meant my mother.

'She one send him bring trouble in my yard. Bwoi, trouble set like rain.'

On the way back to the living room, my eye was drawn to a photo propped up on the mantelpiece next to an ashtray. The framed black-and-white studio portrait of Uncle Percy had probably been on display ever since it was taken, perhaps ten years ago. I must have passed it dozens of times previously, yet it leapt out now. But it wasn't the rakish way Percy wore a trilby that attracted my attention. It was his sheepskin coat.

Percy had aged more than the decade since the photo. All his adult life he'd outpaced the whisky and fags, but they'd caught up with him now. He was bent over with his hands on his thighs, like a long-distance runner at the end of a gruelling marathon. He struggled to catch his breath, on the verge of panic. The finches must have caught something of his mood. They raced around the room excitedly, dropping tiny payloads of shit everywhere. Percy staggered to the kitchen. I thought he was looking for his inhaler, but he returned with a pack of cigarettes. He freed a ciggie from the packet and, answering Betty's silent criticism, reached for the box of matches in his breast pocket. Betty gathered her things immediately. Her movement was resigned and rehearsed. This is the way it always was and always would be. She knew that now. Despite his promises, he was never going to give up. He put the fag to his lips. She fumed. He struck a defiant match. She left.

In her absence, neither of us knew how to begin. Yet the

subject had to be broached. If I felt it, then I'm sure Percy felt it, too.

'Are you related to Virgil in some way?' There could be no doubt, but I asked anyway.

'I don't have no family,' Percy answered drily. 'Your madda like chat people business too much.'

I'd noticed before how some West Indians' patois thickened when they wanted to be raw and direct. They reverted to their natural tongue. 'When it come to family,' said Percy, 'you must eat de fish an' spit out de bone. Dem Adams people is pure bone.'

'He has the Adams nose,' I said.

Percy took a good long draw on the cigarette, right down to the filter, as if he were trying to suck an answer out of it.

'Me gwan tell you somethin' 'bout your madda.' He blew out the final bit of cigarette smoke through the gaps in his clenched teeth. 'You see that mark on she neck?'

My mother had a pronounced birthmark that discoloured her right cheek, which she regularly concealed with make-up. 'The birthmark?'

'That no birthmark. Ethlyn nah born with no mark. No sah, it come from when she a-fool round with one of the dutty servant bwoi. Him have some venereal disease. Don' let the woman fool you!'

It took a while to glean what my grand-uncle was actually saying about his niece, my mother. When I did understand about his unguardedly vindictive and hurtful lie, I struggled, but managed to channel my thoughts into not crying.

After a drawn-out turn once around the block, Betty came back, as both she and Percy knew she would. I was glad she'd returned: there would be no further need to talk. I retreated to my room, nursing ill thoughts about Percy and trying to shake off the idea that I had not defended my mother; and to shut out a voice that whispered 'pathetic' to me as clearly as if someone had snuck in behind me. I drifted off, fighting but eventually giving in to sleep.

In no time, a distant grinding sound woke me, together with the smell of mint and the sense that somebody had entered my bedroom. I opened my eyes. A shadowy grey figure, made up of hundreds of tiny dots – it must have been Percy I suppose – stood over me, crunching on a polo mint. He had a pillow in his hand.

'That pillow a little on the flat side. I bring you another one. Use it, don't use. It's up to you.' Percy let the pillow fall onto the bed and slipped away.

'I no bother answer you,' I answered, but not so loud that he could hear.

I told myself that the imperative to free the birds had nothing to do with the vile lies Percy had told about my mother. After all, what kind of man kept finches? The birds were a little startled when I opened the cage. I should have opened the kitchen window first. I pushed it wide open, but the finches flew everywhere except towards the window; their wings clipped the tips of plates on the draining board and knocked over the neat towers of 50 pence pieces Percy kept on the dining table for the gas and electric meters. I tried vainly to shoo them in the right direction. One disappeared behind the fridge and did not re-emerge. Stuck, I suppose, but you'd have to say it was his own fault. The braver fellow flew out into the night air, but then hovered just outside the window, not knowing what to do with his new-found freedom. I closed the window, tiptoed back to my room and turned off the light. Almost immediately, the light switch was flipped back on in my room.

'What have you done?' barked Percy.

'What do you mean?'

'You know what you've done . . . with the birds. What have you done?'

I couldn't answer.

'Pack your things.'

'What?'

'Now!'

'But I don't have anywhere to go.'

'That's not my concern,' said Percy.

Looking past him into the living room, it appeared as though we'd been burgled. Teacups had been knocked over and smashed onto the floor. Coins were scattered everywhere. The birdcage was open. And from somewhere, it was difficult to work out, but possibly behind the fridge, there was the sound of tapping.

Betty joined Percy at the bedroom door and they both stared unashamedly at me as I filled my case with as much dignity as I could muster. He peeled away, kissing his teeth, but she remained. Betty stayed my hand from continued packing. She told me that she would fix things; that I mustn't leave. I must promise her not to leave. She would fix it.

I lay back on the bed and eventually drifted off, fitfully, once more. It was just as dark when I awoke, as it had been when I'd first gone to bed, but it was evening again now; I'd slept all day. A high screeching sound was coming from the living room and when I wandered out, I saw Percy alone, holding a bow, and slowly drawing it across the strings of a violin that rested in his lap.

'Is that what I think it is?'

Percy didn't look up or answer.

'Is it Aunt Anita's violin?'

'Oh, you heard about that? Is my madda one, yes.'

'Didn't you sell it?'

'Bwoi, stop talk tripe. It look like it sell?'

'People think you sold it.'

'They think wrong.'

'But why didn't you tell them? It would have stopped the consternation, stopped the war.'

'What makes you think I want it stop?' asked Percy.

He picked up the violin, tucked its base under his chin and began to play. I'd like to say that it was remarkable; it wasn't. Percy was a clumsy violinist; his ability was rudimentary, but the effort he made, if not the sound, was mesmerising.

'Let me ask you something,' said Percy, breaking off from playing. 'Suppose you know someone, bring them up even, and they turn out not the way you intended. Would you give them a chance?'

I wasn't sure. I told Percy that I didn't know what he was referring to. But I did really. I knew he had Virgil in mind.

'Do you think you can build them up into what you want them to be?'

I recognised his dilemma in my relationship with Bageye, estranged from us for six years now.

I knew that not only had I released myself from the dream of Bageye's return, but I told myself, as did my siblings, that I didn't want him to return, at least not the man/husband/father he'd become. I knew only this: to preserve the dream you sometimes have to kill it.

If someone, maybe Virgil, had become something other than Percy intended then to hold onto his potential he had to deny him it. Kill it. Maybe the inverse was also true; maybe Virgil felt this about his father. I said none of this to Percy.

'What do you think?' Asked Percy. 'Can you improve them? Build them up into what you want them to be?'

'I don't know. I'm nineteen,' I answered. 'You're a big man. You tell me!'

I was surprised by the sudden sharpness of my voice. But we both knew I had not forgiven him his earlier bitter words about my mother. We surrendered to a neutralising silence, and the longer it persisted the more difficult it became to break. Eventually, Percy stood up, reached for his jacket, put it on and walked towards the door and opened it. He remained like that, with his back to me, as he reminded me that the arrangement had only ever been for me to have a 'cotch' of a few weeks in his spare room, and that those few weeks were up. 'Agreement finish long time, nah so?'

'Yes, it so,' I agreed.

'Good, good,' said Percy. Reaching into his pocket, he pulled out a £20 note, turned and, weighing momentarily the wisdom of the intended gesture, tried to hand the money to me. I refused and, to his credit, Percy did not even attempt to disguise his relief.

'Good. I cyann be hypocrite. It better this way. Cleaner. A clean break, right?' He paused. I sensed he was searching for something meaningful to say – something to remember him by. Finally, he had it: 'Beware the hand that feeds you; you dare not trust your own.'

With that he walked away, pulling the door till it closed gently behind him. From the window I watched him emerge from the block of flats and start to head towards the phone box. Virgil must have sensed him coming. He pushed open the door of the booth, but Percy didn't slow or alter his pace. He kept on walking, staring straight ahead, not looking at the boy in his sheepskin coat.

Selma

Force-ripe gal

Some silences just happen I suppose, like the snow you wake up to that covered the ground whilst you slept. Selma, my big sister and I had hardly spoken in almost a decade. The abrupt end to our communication wasn't intentional: we simply stopped talking. It was like that thing that sometimes happens on a long car journey. Neither the driver nor passenger can quite understand how and why the conversation dribbled away into nothingness. You sit in silence, mile after mile, and the longer the no-talking persists, the more difficult it is to bring to an end.

Following my eviction from Doc Saunders's flat, I didn't seek refuge with Selma, who'd already moved to Maida Vale – a swankier part of London, given its relative proximity to Mayfair, if the Monopoly board was to be believed – some years earlier. Selma was only four years older than me but, throughout our childhood, she'd always seemed more adult than child. Even before she left home, aged eighteen, Selma had become aloof, keeping herself apart from the family, staying long weekends at the plush country homes of her wealthy school friends. Since her departure from Luton, those long weekends had extended into months and then into years. In some sense, you could say, in her self-regard and pursuit of glamour, Selma was not dissimilar to Doc Saunders.

I didn't look for her after leaving Manor House, though over my five years at medical school and beyond, we did meet up occasionally, every few months or so. And then it stopped. From my early thirties for almost a decade, we hadn't spoken.

Maybe the breach between Selma and me was inevitable, even though when growing up, of all the seven siblings, we'd been the most determinedly in each other's corner. That's not strictly true. Selma was more the cornerman than me, and if I was in the ring, on the stool, as it were, and she sensed jeopardy, she'd ignore the figurative bell that sounded 'seconds out'. I'm in trouble? She's not moving out of the ring. Jesus Christ could come down from the Cross, she's still not budging.

I hadn't stopped thinking about Selma, of course, during the last ten years. In fact, she'd featured heavily in a memoir I'd recently written about growing up in Luton, which focused on the year when I was ten. Now, halfway through my interview on Colourful Radio, it was time to discuss Selma. Aged fourteen, my sister, the eldest of us seven, was the kind of child that West Indians, women and men, used to call 'force ripe'. The energetic radio presenter, who sat and fidgeted with his list of questions on the other side of the microphone, was unfamiliar with the phrase. 'Yes,' he said, 'I meant to ask you about that.'

He'd seen it written down in my memoir of growing up in the 1970s on Farley Hill, a council estate in Luton, and had underlined it in the book, bending back the corner of the page. 'What do you mean by "force ripe"?'

'I mean, she was fourteen at the time in which the book is set. But she was mature, like an adult, much earlier than she should have been. You know, when you put a green tomato, say, on the windowsill and you force it to ripen before nature intends.'

'Like bananas?'

'If you like.'

'Or peaches?' chipped in Richard, his co-presenter.

'Yes.'

Their curiosity seemed exaggerated, especially when the main host called for other examples from listeners of force-ripe fruit and the means of their ripening. As he chirped, chivvied and bantered with his co-host, Richard, and listeners, I freed my ears temporarily from the enormous headphones, picked up my copy of the memoir and leafed through it, alighting on Selma's name and stories about her that I hadn't given much thought to since the book's publication.

Before I started to write about my childhood, the past had been full of porous possibilities, an 'open book' that I could rummage through. But in writing – perhaps in a similar way to how a photographic negative submerged in developing fluid slowly and miraculously emerges as a printed record – the past now seemed fixed, and recollections, outside of the memoir, difficult to access. It was a surprise, then, how unbidden memories of Selma drifted and tumbled through my mind amidst the radio show's background chatter. Those remembrances, though, were struggling to compete with the growing presence of Richard.

At the mention of Selma's name, he'd turned towards me, shooting a stolen quizzical glance in my direction. And I was struck by a jolt of recognition about him – a tall, manicured, semi-retired, but still-youthful and excitable advertising executive – that stayed with me for the remainder of the interview.

Afterwards, as we walked to a local cafe in Vauxhall, Richard, who, it transpired, had helped fund the Black community radio station (on condition, I imagined, that he be given the chance to fulfil a lifetime's ambition to be a DJ), claimed to have been confused by my story. During the interview, I'd spoken of growing up poor with siblings, including Selma. For a decade, from the early 1990s this advertising man had worked with an art buyer at Saatchi & Saatchi with a similar-sounding name, Salome.

'How strange! Selma worked for Saatchi & Saatchi as well,' I said, 'but I never knew her job title.'

'You're sure your sister wasn't called Salome?'

'Salome?'

'Yes, Salome. As in, "Bring me the head of John the Baptist."'

'Are you serious? Don't you think I know my sister's name?'

'Of course, sorry, I'm an idiot. I thought, you know, you might have changed it for the book.'

'I didn't.'

'Sorry. Urgh. I'm an idiot.'

Still it was a tantalising thought; there'd been few black women in positions of seniority in the company, Richard told me. But as far as he knew, Salome, his glamorous Saatchi colleague, had not come from an impoverished West Indian family on a Luton council estate, but from a wealthy Ghanaian one, and could best be described as an African princess.

In the photo, conscious of the gap in her upper front teeth, Selma smiles weakly, standing on the steps of our solid brick house. She is neither in nor out. She appears to have assigned herself the role of sentinel. Does her face look welcoming to you? No, all strangers are unwelcome. No one is getting in. Perhaps there's something awful inside, but she is not sparing any would-be caller, she is protecting herself. On the other hand, she may be on her way out, but no one will get sight of what remains behind her until she is well clear, beyond the blast zone, as it were. Perhaps. But then perhaps the picture tells a different story, of an uncomplicated, innocent adolescent, as yet unburdened by shame or censure.

It's 1972 and Selma wears a roughly cut, home-made dress that looks like something picked up at a jumble sale. Ethlyn's many attempts at trying her hand as a seamstress could not be said on this occasion (or any occasion, really), to have been successful. I think the dress is coral-red or salmon pink; it's difficult to tell, as the photo has been colourised by a door-to-door travelling photographer who came to the house. Selma's headband and lips have been colourised, too, it seems, to match the dress. My sister is fourteen but looks five years older. Barely into her teens, you'd have said Selma was the acme of force ripe.

To me, though just four years older, she was almost regal, walking around the estate as if the residents of Farley Hill were her subjects. Even our father, Bageye, seemed to contract, reduced in her presence. 'Watch her now,' he'd snort, when most vexed by his adolescent daughter. 'She comin' like the Queen.' The way she carried herself, her poise, was hard-earned in part from hours of walking around the house with the Yellow Pages telephone directory balanced on her head. But it was more than that. Selma seemed to glide through life, as if by rights you ought to be grateful to be graced by her company. I *was* grateful, mostly; though alongside my siblings, I secretly suspected that after Selma's birth, our parents must have been taken to the wrong crib. She never seemed to belong; she didn't even look like any of us, not really. She had more the look and feel of the Adamses, Ethlyn's family, than the Grants.

The cafe was little more than a greasy spoon, but had spruced itself up a little bit to take advantage of Vauxhall's changing demographic, offering soya lattes now, along with fancy-sounding bagels. Essentially, though, it was a greasy spoon (all tables came with bottles of vinegar and ketchup in a red, plastic dispenser shaped like a giant tomato), and hadn't yet alienated the regulars who still came in for a fry-up, followed by a fag.

Richard emptied sachet after sachet of sugar into his coffee, so much that he had trouble stirring it.

'I've this funny feeling we've met before,' he said.

'You're sure you don't want another sachet?'

'This is me cutting down,' he laughed, continuing to stir. Finally, he tapped the side of the cup with the spoon. 'We've met before, I'm sure of it.'

I confessed that I, too, had the same feeling, but couldn't specify a time or place.

'What do you do again? BBC, wasn't it?'

'Trying not to let it define me,' I smiled.

'And before?'

'There's no before or after once Auntie gets a grip,' I said.

'Law? Law school?'

'Nope.'

'Banking? Weren't you something in the City?'

'Your father want see you,' Ethlyn said distractedly, as I wandered through the kitchen which was 'closed by the way', my mother informed me, as she continued cooking on the stove. 'Gwan about your business, that man asking for you.'

'What about?'

She must have heard the alarm in my voice but volunteered no further information. 'Stop puke around!' She snapped at the sight of my suddenly sagging shoulders and went back to turning the heavy spoon in the pot and seasoning the pigtail soup that never managed to approximate being edible. 'Quick time!' said Ethlyn. 'You only mek it worse.'

But I knew I was not the cause of her irritation; Ethlyn was 'taking Selma fat fry me'. My sister was gwan with her facety self, taking her sweet time putting on her house clothes, as directed, and taking off the orange party dress that Ethlyn had sweated over in making. Selma had recently started wearing the dress around the house as she'd no intention of stepping out the yard in that God-awful thing. She'd only reluctantly put it on for the photographer, *as instructed* by Ethlyn, because there was no other dressing-up dress.

I didn't want an audience for my expected humiliation by Bageye, but, ignoring my protests, Selma followed me, like a priest, on my long gallows' march to Bageye's bedroom. Outside of Ladbrokes and Coral, my father's bedroom was where all his most important decisions were made, and especially punishments given. Selma's jaunty manner, struck for my benefit, nonetheless failed to mask her concern. It was only when we reached the top of the stairs that I realised I'd been holding – no, squeezing – her hand. She had to peel my palm away and nudge me gently towards the bedroom. I walked in alone, but she stayed at the door peering through the crack in the frame.

Bageye sat on the edge of the bed, busying himself with his tobacco tin, cigarette papers and the cute miniature rolling-pin thingy that never failed to produce a perfectly neat cigarette. The rolling was a reflex, though; this afternoon he seemed only half-committed to smoking. My father had his back to me but, as I edged further into the room, he coughed, 'Is you, that?' I stared ahead, looking at the curtained window and the fine dust of particles caught in the dying light. In the late-afternoon gloom, my thoughts were drawn towards the narrow windowsill. I was tempted to leap up and sit on it, something I'd often done when Bageye wasn't around; I loved the elevation of sitting high up there, and the challenge, the near impossibility of achieving it. For a moment, I worried that my father could read my thoughts, but he didn't look up; Bageye appeared to be directing most of his thinking inside the dank confines of that tobacco tin.

'You remember what I say to you that time?'

I didn't need reminding. We'd been warned incessantly by Bageye that he didn't ever, ever want to see one of his pickney, not one of them, playing fool for the white man. For the last twenty-four hours, I'd been fearing the revelation that I'd failed his instruction. Bageye had turned up at the Catholic social club the night before, during an exhibition boxing match, to be confronted with the sight of me in the ring.

'You were being watched, fool. You think you're not being watched?' Bageye was dismayed. This had always been his mantra to us growing up. He didn't mean he had his eye on us; rather he was alerting us to the cold fact that we were under surveillance by the neighbours and society at large. As the children of black Jamaican migrants, we were being watched by the host nation of curtain-twitchers to see how we turned out, simple so; to see whether we conformed to the stereotype they had of us as being work-shy simpletons, destined for a life of crime. Our father would descend on us regularly with this sermon, jabbing his finger at each of us in turn.

The truth of Bageye's thinking was backed up by the casual, overheard remarks of teachers and neighbours that the best that could be hoped for us 'poor things' was that we'd one day make a living as entertainers, most likely in sport. Bageye was adamant that we should fool them and have the last laugh – 'mek dem stay there laugh.' I'd nodded, but secretly defied my father: I joined the boxing club. And the day before, tipped off by a neighbour, he'd turned up at the exhibition match, to see me scrambling to remove my boxing gloves to scoop up coins thrown into the ring by the appreciative – and all-white – crowd. Sufferin' succotash!

'So why you do that t'ing, after me done tell you already?'

Bageye waited, but I couldn't answer. I felt my mouth was full of pebbles.

'You don't have tongue in your head?'

'No, no, no! You don't have to be so rough with him.' Selma answered for me, through the gap in the door. 'No need to be so rough.'

'I talking to you?' Bageye yelled.

'But he hasn't done anything.'

'Stop run your mout' gal.'

'He hasn't done anything wrong.'

'I talking to you?'

Bageye flicked his hand, directing Selma to be gone, but she didn't budge. She wasn't going to leave, even if there were likely consequences for her later on; she would act as witness to whatever was coming. Bageye cussed some more, and glared at me, heavy with disappointment.

'You is a common-sense man. You is my likkle common-sense man.'

The sound of each 'common-sense' was like a nail tapped further, resoundingly, into a piece of wood. 'You suppose to have more common sense!'

We both fell silent. The pebbles may have dropped from my mouth, but my tongue now cleaved to its roof.

'Don't mek me and you have argument again. You understand?'

I nodded, and blinked back the tears that were threatening to form.

'You have good brains,' said Bageye eventually. His voice

35

softened. He told me that he hadn't slept well. He'd been thinking and thinking and thinking. All night, after the boxing match, he'd been troubled by what it meant that I had 'good brains'. Just like that the answer had come to him; and bwoi, when it hit, he couldn't just roll over and go back to sleep.

'I feel you gwan be a doctor,' said Bageye. He spoke gravely, and yet his voice was tinged with a kind of self-regarding pleasure, perhaps at the wondrousness of his revelation, at the majesty of it. It wasn't the first time that my future had been discussed. Recently, I'd passed the entrance exam to an expensive private school, but Bageye was yet to work out the fees situation, whether it was even possible as there was only one wage coming into the house and plenty pickney to feed and clothe, not to mention his one little twice-weekly pleasure at the bookies.

And there were, of course, the further complications that my brother Milton had also passed the entrance exam, and that Selma was already in her third year at St Francis College for Girls where the cost of the uniform alone was enough to make a grown man faint. I wasn't sure I was supposed to reply to the doctor business. Once again, Selma intervened, whispering through the crack: 'He can be whatever he wants to be.'

It seemed then such a strange, unforgettable thing to say, although not for Selma, I suppose. I'd never considered the idea before that you could be absolutely anything you wanted to be. I'd never forget the optimism of that assertion. I can see now that not only did Selma believe it, *actually* believe it, but every decision she made was toward that end point for herself. 'You can turn yourself into whatever you want to be' would be *the* code by which she lived. My father appeared not to hear, so Selma repeated her taunt until Bageye thundered back: 'He gwan be a doctor!'

By this point, I'd reached the wardrobe, a big bulky affair whose extraordinarily heavy doors were peculiarly and fascinatingly, to us kids, held in place by a pair of flimsy, retractable pins at either end. Selma and I had once fantasised (her idea, really) about loosening the pins and making enough noise to lure Bageye up to the bedroom just in time for a lethal wardrobe door to slip its pins and come crashing down on him. Occasionally, we'd revisit the fantasy, imagining ourselves his cartoon nemeses scheming to reduce him to smithereens, even as we understood, sadly, that come crunch time our father was always likely to nonchalantly take a step to one side just as Bugs Bunny did in the 'Looney Tunes' cartoons whenever a deadly boulder, levered off a cliff's edge by his enemy, plummeted towards him.

I caught Selma's eye through the door's crack. Her eyes flicked left to right and back again between the bed and the wardrobe, as if she was issuing some kind of code. I knew what she was hinting at, but there was no chance now. Bageye remained on the edge of the bed, out of harm's way. Finally, he lit the cigarette. For all his faults, Bageye was a man like this: when a strange and powerful thought came to him, even if it was to prove personally detrimental, he could not turn away from it. I suppose sending three kids to expensive private schools was Bageye's impossibly high windowsill that he'd be in perpetual danger of slipping from. What a blast.

'What if he doesn't want to be a doctor?' asked Selma.

'That is not the question.'

'It's *a* question.'

'But not *the* question.'

'Why don't you ask *him*?'

'Him? Is so you speak to your father? Cha!'

My father firmly fixed me in his gaze and said: 'I feel you gwan be a doctor. Yes man, I feel it!'

And that was it. Whilst we younger siblings were beguiled by Selma, and were amazed by her spirited challenges to our father (even Bageye would concede about his eldest child: 'That gal not easy, you know'); ultimately if Bageye said a thing was so, then it was so.

It appeared ordained, even, when later that Saturday afternoon, we kids all crammed onto the settee in the back room to watch a film. Usually it would have been some dreadful musical we'd be forced by Selma to watch. I say 'forced', but actually Selma had a way of remote-controlling me that meant I did her bidding, a tradition that would continue into my early adulthood; she wouldn't get up from the settee but, with a sweep of her hand, she'd direct me to change the channel amidst protests from the others, as if it was *my* decision. Thankfully, it wasn't *Seven Brides for Seven Brothers* or *Oklahoma!* on the telly this time but something that was met with universal approval.

A famous actor, a man who always made us feel better about ourselves and the race, appeared in a Spencer Tracy and Katharine Hepburn movie. We admired the sweet old, liberal-hearted white couple, Tracy and Hepburn. But we loved, absolutely loved Sidney Poitier. *Guess Who's Coming to Dinner* was thrilling because of Poitier's character, Dr John Prentice, a high-minded medical doctor who was immaculate in every way: delightful manners; manicured fingernails; starched, brilliant-white collar and cuffs; and an elegant suit. Selma came at it a little differently. Most important, as far as she was concerned, was not that brother number one was black, but that Dr Prentice was in conflict with his father over his attempt to control and limit his son. Selma leapt on a line in the film where the young doctor berates his father: 'Not until your whole generation has lain down and died will the dead weight of you be off our backs!' She raised an eyebrow to me, as if to say 'you see, you see,' repeating the doctor's line. That same afternoon whenever Bageye passed by or made his presence known, Selma would whisper to us, 'dead weight'. Later she took me aside to tell me, as was her way, what was what: 'By all means little man, become a doctor, if that's what you really want but not because of dead weight. Do you see?'

I didn't see; yet the idea of challenging any of Selma's assertions always filled me with the same kind of dread I felt about the prospect of being caught out answering back to Bageye. I *could* see that Selma had a blind spot when it came to our father, and he to her.

'I remember now,' said Richard. 'Weren't you at dental school or something?'

'Well you've been through every other profession. What's left?'

'Medical school! The London Hospital? Joseph Merrick. The Elephant Man. The London Hospital, right?'

'It's the Royal London Hospital now.'

'Finally!' Richard's face cleared with satisfaction. 'Now we're getting somewhere.'

'You carry on bad!' I said tartly. 'This is not a joke, joke t'ing you know, bredren.'

Richard suddenly blushed with discomfort. He was perplexed, not just by my Home Counties patois, but by the unexpected coldness of my tone. Annoyingly, as was usually the case in such circumstances, having hooked him out of the comforts of his water, as it were, I felt a kind of pity and let him go.

'It's what my Uncle Castus says. Life's not a game. "It's not a joke, joke t'ing."'

'I know, I know,' Richard said, raising his hand with the

39

laminated menu, trying to catch the waiter's attention. 'Don't you want to know how we, you know, know each other?'

'I did, an hour ago. But maybe it's time to get on with the rest of my life.'

'Do you have a picture of Selma? That's her name, right? Do you have a picture?'

I shook my head. But even if I'd had a picture, I wouldn't have shown it to him. I felt there was a third person at the table whispering to me, 'Tell him nothing. Let him be disappointed. Tell him nothing, not one thing.'

Bageye stood at the ironing board, pressing his suit trousers nice, nice (bwoi, those creases were sharp enough to cut!) before moving on to a brilliant-white shirt (Bageye was heavy on the starch) and a couple of ties (he hadn't made a decision yet for the night's Blues party; the man needed options: he would see how he felt last minute). But, as far as Ethlyn was concerned and let us know, if Bageye thought he was just going to waltz out of the house, and 'leave me and you pickney to stew, whilst he shake up he-self at the Blues party with the dutty, blue-foot Irish gal-dem on the dance floor, then he better think again, to rahted!' If he thought that, he could kiss her backside.

No sooner had her husband finished smoothing out the final tie and heavy-handedly started to pack away the ironing board than Ethlyn shouted up to the bedroom and told him to 'leave the t'ing there, right there. You finish, but me just start.' And she cursed under her breath, 'Yes, run to your blue foot! Nasty naygar.'

If Bageye thought he'd managed to get clean away from his miserable family, then he was mistaken. Ethlyn told us to go upstairs, to take off of our house clothes and put on our good clothes, our Sunday suits and frocks. Pretty soon we were filing out of the house.

'One time I had three in a pram and one walking,' said Ethlyn, as we struggled to match her pace down the hill.

'I take it I was never in a pram, then?' Selma interrupted before our mother could build on her story. 'Doesn't surprise me. I was born to walk. We come from a long line of walkers, right, Mum?'

'I never even bother answer you,' answered Ethlyn.

'What's the hurry? What are we going to do once we get there? Probably be shoved away in a corner somewhere. I can't wait.' Selma held out her arms pleading, 'Mother, what's the point of this, again?'

At moments like this, I worried that my big sister was a fantasist (although I'd not have known that word). She took more notice of the cocktail set who populated *The Betsy*, the latest, slightly trashy book by a writer called Harold Robbins she loved to read, than the reality all around her; and I feared that maybe, in spite of her brilliance, she was soft in the brain for not seeing or caring that there was always a price to be paid for her impudence.

Selma wilfully misunderstood the point of Ethlyn dressing up all of her pickney in their Sunday-best church dresses and suits (Selma was forced to wear the orange gown) to head out of their yard on a cold night, to turn up at a party on big, big Saturday night, where they most likely would not be welcome, or at least would be made to feel unwelcome. Selma didn't understand that the point was that Ethlyn had made up her mind. 'Stop long down your mout',' Ethlyn berated us. We were going to the party, where it would be Ethlyn's little chance for fun, whether we enjoyed it or not.

On the way down Long Croft Road, Selma slipped from 'Mummy' to 'Mum' to 'Mother' without making any impression. She only stopped with her veiled nagging when Ethlyn concluded to no one in particular, but loud enough for everyone to hear: 'Girl child? You should drown them at birth.'

It may have sounded a little harsh, but Ethlyn didn't really mean it. Not *really*, really. She'd said it before, of course, and sometimes I wondered whether that was really the point of Selma's provocation – to get our mum to say it, so Selma could harden her heart against her. In any event, there, it was said.

Although there was no more talk from Selma, she had seeded doubt in some of us other children; there were calls for turning back and one or two began a go-slow the closer we got to our destination. Having inspired a mini-mutiny, though, Selma ploughed on, and in doing so, silently encouraged our well-dressed ragtag outfit to follow her lead.

We heard the Blues party, already in full swing, as we turned the corner onto Tennyson Road. In the last few minutes and steps towards the house Selma seemed to have settled into the conviction that the real enemy, for now anyway, was not she who had given birth to her; the real enemy was inside the house. Yes man, Bageye loved to party and he'd have been there from time, stoking the fire, offering advice on the curry goat, liberating a chicken leg from the pot, preparing the rum punch. As Ethlyn attended to some last-minute adjustments to our clothes, Selma forged ahead like a big person and, much to our horror, climbed the steps, not to the back door, but to the front.

The Adams family – our grandmother Pauline and an ever-changing number of her adult children who'd led a middle-class life in Jamaica – all lived together at Tennyson Road, an acceptable, if not sought-after, residential area of Luton. Over the years it had become a kind of haven for West Indians in Luton, known for its Blues parties, which the elderly matriarch always attended, even though she'd be asleep in a chair much of the time. Frail and slight, Pauline was actually a pathological assassin (of character), an ever-smiling, but scary figure who never spoke above a whisper, and who reigned over the house through intrigue, scheming and setting her adult children one against the other. An out-of-favour uncle or aunt (and there was always one of those) would be ostracised by the rest of the clan for a while before working out how to get back into the fold.

The Adams family held Bageye in low regard but, oddly, held their own Ethlyn in even lower regard, so that you could have mistakenly believed that they had a fondness for Bageye. It all had something to do with my grandmother's jealousy of Ethlyn, who had been her own father's favourite. Why Ethlyn's siblings went along with this madness was never clear to me. At least their disregard did not *fully* extend to her children, although there was always something discomfiting about Granny Adams's veiled antipathy towards her oldest grandchild. Selma didn't want to believe it – at some level she was enthralled by the Adams people, and got on famously with Adriene, Pauline's youngest child, who at nineteen was close enough in age to forge an inseparable bond with Selma – but Granny Adams was somehow also jealous of Selma.

The Adams family may have considered Ethlyn and her brood to be the pitiably poor relations, who, slumming in a council house on the Farley Hill estate, exhibited the kind of life that back home in Jamaica would have been considered servant class; but that was not a descriptor that Selma recognised in herself. Like many of the Adams folk, Selma would have considered being called a snob a compliment. She knocked on the front door and, of course, Bageye answered. Our father sighed. Beneath the knotty frown you could see his mind racing. But no words came out of that harsh throat. The sight of Selma was too much for the poor man. He and his wife had never gotten along; he could manage that, but on occasion, it must have felt, with Selma in Ethlyn's corner, that they had ganged up and out-manoeuvered him. Even before it had warmed up, Bageye must have felt the party was 'spoil already'.

Bageye looked beyond his number-one child, out at all the progeny that he had regretfully begot with 'that woman' in more than a decade of unending unhappiness. Without saying a word, Bageye retreated into the bowels of the Adams house, and like an occupying force that had breached enemy lines, Selma called us forward, swarming through the open front door.

Once inside, unsurprisingly, we were shepherded into an overspill room that seemed to have been designated for coats. But what was unexpected was that Ethlyn soon disappeared as well. I hadn't thought till then just how exciting it must have been for her to be around her siblings once more, even if they pitied her, to have the chance to talk some old-time talk, to remember what they were, truly were, or had been in Jamaica, and not what they had become in England.

'Me soon come,' Ethlyn had said, but thirty minutes and then an hour passed with no sign of her.

I don't recall anyone coming in with a camera that evening. But there is a black-and-white snapshot of us startled pickney, all crammed into two armchairs, stiff in coarse tweed suits and home-made dresses, perfectly capturing our collective misery. All that is, except Selma, who is laughing in the photo, stretched out with two little ones on her knees.

Eventually we volunteered Selma to go on a reconnaissance sortie. She came back shortly after, hurriedly and laughing. There was someone following her.

'Your children are thirsty,' said Selma, when Bageye put his head around the door and peered into the room, empty except for us, squeezed into the two chairs.

'Where that woman gwan?'

'Wherever our mother is, your children still need food and drink; they're dead fi hungry.'

'Who put you in charge?' asked Bageye.

The beginnings of a smile leaked from the corners of Selma's lips. Our father's question was an admission of defeat.

'Monkey do as monkey see.'

'Why you have to talk so? Why? Tell me why. Why I send you go private school, work double shift, all for you to end up speak like me? Me, who don't even pass worms.'

'I couldn't really say,' Selma answered. 'Spite?'

Bageye backed out of the room and slammed the door closed with such force, I feared he must now be standing on the other side of the door, holding the separated handle. It was sad how people always fell into a way of being or defaulted to an irreversible way of seeing. I wished Bageye could see Selma as I did, because often her haughty manner was just a product of her mischievous character, which was not unlike his; it wasn't spite, it was enjoyment. I could see that, and I was only ten. What Bageye didn't appreciate was what most amused us about Selma: her mimicry. She was equally at home sounding as posh as a well-heeled, upper-middle-class girl as she was mimicking the raw patois of a low-class higgler woman from Jamaica. Today we'd call it code-switching. Back then it must have seemed bizarre. She certainly wrong-footed the big people when she smoothly switched from the Queen's English into speaking just like them.

Five minutes passed. Nothing. Ten minutes passed before a stranger, a white woman, entered with a tray of Coca-Cola bottles, followed by her friend with a tray of bun and cheese. They both 'ahhed' at the sight of us in our smart clothes and quietness; they set down the trays, mission completed, and left.

'Blue foot,' Selma whispered when they'd gone – which was a bit unfair. Most Saturday nights when Bageye prepared for an evening of socialising – ironing his shirt, a splash of after shave and dash of mouth spray – Ethlyn would curse him as he headed out the door, 'Yes, run to your blue foot.' We worked out that a blue foot was a poor white lady whose legs, because she didn't wear tights in the winter, turned blue in the chilly breeze. Perhaps the women with the trays wore too much make-up and were heavy on the perfume, but they were nice, they didn't have to bring us bun and cheese, I argued.

'I'm not disputing that,' said Selma. 'You can be both Madonna and whore, that's all.' Selma had brought along the nail polish kit she'd saved up for over several weeks and was practising using it now. She looked up, distracted by our silence. 'Nothing wrong with that; it's just how the cards fall.'

Once we'd wolfed down the drinks and bun and cheese, everyone agreed on the need for seconds. Selma picked up a tray, balancing the empty bottles and gestured, with a tilt of her head, for me to accompany her with the other tray of empty plates.

Out in the hallway, Bageye, a cigarette in one hand and a glass of Guinness in the other, held forth with a group of men. I only recognised Clock who'd gone full 'Superfly' for the party with a paisley shirt and brown suede jacket with lapels wide enough for a plane to take off from. Bageye was running jokes with Clock, which was funny because, generally, even he'd agree, Clock was mean and had no sense of humour. At every opportunity people always used to ask Clock, who had one arm longer than the other, the correct time. But there was no point because he never wore a watch. We sensed that there was something more than nasty about Clock; a lacking in the morals department. The drinks and vibes must have gotten the better of the men, especially Clock, because they were talking above the music, loud enough to be heard.

'Is she, dat?' We heard Clock burp as we approached with the trays. 'She turn big woman.'

'Yes, man, me have two of dem now. She and the mother.'

'Bwoi, that nah easy.'

'Eeeh eeh.'

'She well ripe,' said another man. 'Ripe as a Julie mango.'

The men laughed hard; Clock hardest of all. Selma put down the tray beside his feet. She brushed and straightened her dress and addressed Clock: 'Say that again.'

Clock simply swilled the ice in his glass of rum.

'You don't have any shame?'

'Me?' Clock slapped the man closest to him on the shoulder: 'If me have for pay for all the things me done wrong in this here world, well boss, me have one bitch of a bill a-come.'

Selma turned to Bageye. 'What about you?'

Our father didn't say a word. Worse, Bageye looked at her as if *he* was the one that had been offended; his eyes were as cold as a new razor blade. I could feel my stomach churning. Whatever was said next was critical. It would be best to not say *anything* but I knew Selma was not minded to hold her sharp tongue, even when big people were present.

It was a relief and a surprise, when ignoring the adults, she spoke directly to me: 'Go fetch your mother. I think the party's over.' Selma commanded me to put the tray down beside hers, right there on the floor, but I struggled with it through to the kitchen. Ethlyn was propped up by the stove, sipping a Babycham and giggling. Immediately she saw me, my mother put

47

down her drink. I didn't have to give her any message; Ethlyn could tell something was off and followed me straight away to the hallway and then into the overspill room. She swept up the others, helped them on with their coats, and we headed out into the street.

That night I dreamed of my father's destruction, but Bageye was indestructible; some people just are. Bageye resided in the house, but lived mostly upstairs in his bedroom. I say 'lived', but I mean festered and stewed over whatever plots he imagined Ethlyn was hatching and filling the pickneys' heads with. When roused by any sound downstairs, he'd descend to berate, instruct or generally just terrorise us. Collectively, we were Jack and he was the fearful giant. The stairs were our beanstalk and from time to time Selma would encourage us to loosen the clips on the carpet runner so that, on his way down, Bageye would trip and break his neck; he never did. Our father had an uncanny sense for when things were not quite right – whether the position of the lavatory seat or the smoothness of the stair-case carpet. Listening out for when he descended the stairs, there'd be a moment of silence and suddenly no more steps. We'd hurry expectantly from the back room to find him, not prostrate at the bottom, but halfway up, bent over fixing a clip on the stairs and straightening the carpet.

We heard Bageye come down those stairs the next day, and each step deepened our foreboding. He ignored Ethlyn, waving her away as if she were a mosquito, which he knew he'd never swat, but which he realised, too, could do no serious harm. Bageye had no desire to place his order for breakfast, thank you; the ackee and saltfish could wait. He planted his feet on the floor of the back room; his eyes drilled into the back of Selma's head; she made a point of not turning around. One of them would have to make the first move. But that decision was further deferred by the thud of the door-knocker sounding firmly on the front door.

'Ah who that now?' asked Ethlyn. At such times it was always easy to read her frown as she ran through a quick mental inventory of whom she owed money to, before speedily concluding that the candidates never changed; she still owed money to everyone – the milkman, the council for the rent, the hire-purchase collector, the money lender, a neighbour or two. As the least likely to object, I was selected by Ethlyn, to go and investigate the knocking. I hesitated. Bageye continued to stare at Selma; she still refused to turn from her important work, painting her nails. The knock sounded again, more persistently.

'Go on, you won't miss anything.' said Selma. 'We won't start without you.' I was too fearful to move, feeling that she wanted to spare me from the awfulness of what was about to unfold, to give me licence, coward that I was, to flee the danger zone.

'When does this start?' Selma asked evenly, still with her back to Bageye and the room. 'Whatever this is. What are we waiting for?' And as I scrambled out of the settee, knocking knees with the others, Selma shouted, 'Tell them I won't be long.'

'Tell them? Who's them?'

'Them. At the door. I won't be long.'

I sped down the hallway but even before I reached the door, I heard the commotion beginning in the back room; it sounded like Bageye was barking. I waited, my hand on the lock, for a lull in the shouting. When I pulled open the front door, there were three young white girls all aged about fourteen, all as pale and bleached as the sky, shoulder to shoulder on the step.

Something about their pristine look and poise reminded me of the highly groomed racehorses we saw on TV paraded before the race; their voices were clipped but warm. I wasn't surprised to hear that they were school friends of Selma from St Francis College; they had her same unnerving assuredness. But there was nothing shadowing their lives; they looked serene.

What were they doing here, though? Their presence was bewildering; not simply because no one like them had ever appeared magically at our doorstep, but also the fact that Selma would never have countenanced giving these upper-middle-class girls our council house address. Selma was self-conscious about the contrast between our circumstances and that of the well-to-do families of her fee-paying peers.

The perfect manners of Selma's friends – they'd come to collect her on the way to a party – was drowned out by the renewed fracas in the back room. They were too polite to register or signal that they heard Bageye agitatedly and loudly reminding their friend not to get too comfortable: 'If you can do better than my house, then just move your backside.' Neither did they comment on Selma's retort to Bageye: 'It's not your house; it's the council's. You don't own it. In fact, what do you own? Nothing. Nothing. Nothing.'

I made an attempt at an explanation about what was going on, to say something, anything, but it was beyond me. We all heard the sound of drawers being roughly opened and Selma's continued taunt: 'Because you gamble away the money. Because you're a small man with no ambition.'

There was another barely distinguishable but dreadful sound of someone rummaging through drawers of cutlery. Perhaps.

'Can you get Selma for us?' One of the girls asked. There were three of them, but they were basically the same person. 'She's expecting us.'

'I think you have the wrong house,' I said.

Throughout their time on the doorstep, the argument had been rising in the back room.

'Isn't that her voice?' Just as the girl asked, there was a loud piercing shriek. It was sudden and shocking. I wasn't sure what was happening but left the girls on the doorstep and hurried to the back room.

My brothers and sisters were wailing; Ethlyn screamed and pleaded with her husband. Bageye sat in the armchair. Selma was on his knee but not upright; she kind of flopped as if having surrendered after a struggle. Breathing heavily, Bageye had his daughter in an arm lock and her fingers (with recently manicured and painted nails), held tightly in his hand. In his other hand, Bageye held a pair of scissors.

'Where are you gwan with them claw? You gwan out my yard, so? A-fling you would like fling them claw in my face?' He took the scissors and cut off her fingernails. Selma offered no resistance as he switched to her other hand and cut the nails off those fingers, too. When he was done, both were too exhausted to move; they remained – Bageye appeared weirdly to be cradling her – in the armchair, parent and adult-child like a perversion of Michelangelo's *Pietà*.

No one could look in their direction but it was agony, too, to avert your gaze. Somehow I edged myself out of the room and found my way back to the front door. But there was no one on the doorstep or to the side or down the alley; the polite girls had slipped away.

'What was your name again? Grant?'

'Yes.'

'Well that's funny? Salome was Adams-Grant.'

'Arh.'

'Arh? Hold on. Adams? Adams?' Richard picked up his copy of my book. 'Isn't there an Adams family in your memoir?' He found what he was looking for in the book, and left it open on the page on the table, sliding it towards me, as if showing his hand in a game of poker.

'People are entitled to their privacy.' I said.

'You're a writer for God's sake. What are you talking about? It was your mother's maiden name, right?'

Richard was enjoying himself. He held back, though, from spelling out his conclusion. Perhaps he was disturbed by my fierce silence.

The lights were out in the bedroom we all shared. Though nothing was said, we seemed to have reached an agreement not to mention the afternoon business of scissors and nails. There were no tears from Selma; her voice was flecked with rage, over 'the evil wretch' who had fathered us with as much thought as a man blowing snot into his handkerchief. Selma vowed never to speak to Bageye again, not one word. The bathroom sink was out of bounds too, to be boycotted because in that same basin where she washed her face, 'the evil wretch washes his thing'. She would have no cause for using the sink again because she was not spending another night in this house, you hear. 'Horse can dead, cow can fat, you not seeing me in this house. No sir, when you don't see me I gone.'

Selma was lighting out for the territory and anyone who was smart enough could join her. There were no volunteers. She assured us that we were all doomed, but never mind, and fumbling in the dark, she started to gather her things. She picked up my duffel bag and I objected. When she countered that it was only 'a borrows', that I'd have it back one day, and that in the meantime, it'd be something to remember me by, I pleaded with her not to go.

'Don't be silly,' said Selma. 'I have no choice.'

'But why must you go?'

'I must.'

'Is it because of what happened?'

When she didn't answer, I said I was sorry.

'You didn't do anything.'

'Exactly, I didn't do *anything*.'

Selma came to my side of the bed, reached for my comb, and ran it through my hair. I started to cry, but not so loud that I'd disturb the others.

'It's not your fault. You're not the enemy. Remember who the enemy is.' She told me to close my eyes, and then kissed my eyelids.

'Better?'

I nodded and shook away the remaining tears.

'So where are you going?'

'Going to foreign.'

'What, to one of those girls' houses?'

'All the way to Welwyn Garden City? Nah, too far.'

'Where then?'

'Monkey know which tree fi climb . . . Where do you think?'

'Tennyson Road?'

I reminded Selma that she didn't really like the Adams woman who called herself our granny, and who presided over her weird cult at Tennyson Road. Selma agreed, but added that one day I'd understand that when you're a big person, you have to be practical. 'Eat the fish and spit out the bones.'

She crept out of the bedroom, waving one last time. As soon as the front door clicked, I jumped out of bed and went to inform Ethlyn who didn't seem surprised, not one bit. She stifled a yawn, and pulled the blanket back over her shoulder.

'What if she doesn't come back?' I asked.

'There'll be one less mouth to feed.'

With that, Ethlyn turned onto her side and pretended to go back to sleep.

I saw in that gesture that my mother's indifference was a mask of disappointment, and an awareness that the future that she had long held out against would come to pass; that her children, first Selma and then the rest of us, would leave her one by one until she was all alone. I saw, too, at that moment, that Selma's leave-taking would not be successful, but that it was a rehearsal for what was to come. Ethlyn used to assert that there were few things in life that were non-negotiable; allegiance to family was number one. But just because you share the same blood as someone doesn't mean you have anything more in common with them other than your bloodline; indeed you can hate them for it, as Selma would find out later that night.

If Granny Adams hated our mother (there was never really any doubt about it), that was as nothing compared to her apparent fear and resentment of Selma's influence over, and proximity to, our aunt Adriene.

I wasn't sure how long it was after the pretence of sleep – maybe an hour, maybe two – before Ethlyn had jumped out of bed, dressed quickly and shot out of the house for Tennyson Road.

Selma would recount, when she returned that night with Ethlyn, how she'd been put in the same room as Adriene, and had fallen asleep, only to wake up half-dazed to find Pauline looming over her with a pillow in her hands. Pauline had intended to smother her granddaughter with the pillow. Our granny would later claim that Selma had just had a terrible dream; Granny

Adams, by her account, had come into the bedroom to find the pillow on the floor and had just picked it up when Selma opened her eyes. Selma knew otherwise. She never believed Granny Adams, never went back to Tennyson Road, and bided her time before she could leave Farley Hill forever, a few years later.

'You know, I have Salome's number in my phone.' Richard took out his mobile. 'We could call her now.' He tapped in a number and put the phone to his ear.

'Please don't,' I said, and he ended the call before the connection was made.

'Such a shame,' said Richard. He asked for the bill, and the waiter wandered over slowly, tore off a sheet from his pad and placed it face down on our table. 'In your own time,' he said.

For the want of somewhere else to look other than Richard's supercilious face, I focused uncharitably on his purple pork-pie hat that hadn't left his head since the radio studio. It seemed an affectation now, worn self-consciously as a signature of cool.

Richard's phone rang. 'Do you mind?' he asked, tapping on the screen without waiting for me to answer. A smile wrapped quickly around his delighted face. 'Sssss, hello! Yes, that was me. We've just been talking about you. At least, I think we have. Anyway, there's someone here I'm sure would like a word. Hold on, caller.'

Richard held out his phone. I could hear the squeak of a voice coming from it. I let him hold out the phone for as long as I could until it was clear that he would not relent. The familiar voice continued to squeak. Richard smirked as I took his bloody phone and pressed the red button, shutting off the call.

Bageye

Blood mus' follow vein

Repairing the breach with Selma would come when it came, I told myself. It was not impossible to conceive, or at least not as impossible as any reunion with Bageye. Yet just a couple of years before that non-telephone exchange with my sister, I'd set to one side my resolution never to be reunited with the man we children and our mother had called 'Satan', 'the evil wretch' or 'pathetic' – Selma's description of choice.

Bageye was surprisingly easy to find when I set out to track him down. I simply rang The Chequers, the main West Indian pub in Luton that he'd always frequented. 'Can you help? I'm looking for Clinton Grant,' I asked. The pub's landlady turned the name over with her tongue as she thought, but the name didn't register.

'What him look like?'

I described my father's most pronounced feature: the permanent bags under his eyes.

'Oh, you mean Bageye. Wait a second.' I heard her lift the hatch on the bar and shuffle along; some old-time ska played in the background. A minute or so passed before she returned to the phone. 'He's here now,' said the landlady. 'You want I is to put him on?'

I slammed down the receiver.

The next day I rang The Chequers again to apologise to the landlady, who called herself Mrs Paulette, to explain that I hadn't expected my father to be there; it'd been too soon for me to speak with Bageye. I was caught off guard, I said. Mrs Paulette was kindly and amused, laughing through her dry smoker's cough as I spoke. She said she'd anticipated that I'd phone back, but I was talking too quickly for her.

'Give me a second, nah. What them call you?'

I hesitated, before eventually settling for Craig, my middle name, and the one I'd mostly been called as a child in Luton.

'Creg?'

'No. Craig.'

'Yes, Creg. I remember Creg! So you is Bageye son? Sound just like Country.'

'Country?'

'Yes man, Country.'

'I sound like someone called Country?'

'How you is Bageye son and you nah know Country?' I heard her turning over what sounded like papers. 'You *is* Bageye son?'

I let the question hang in the air. Anyway, she was too distracted, leafing through a book or pad or whatever it was, to ask for a third time. She had Bageye's address written down – given by him – ready for me. Did I want it? It was a good question. 'You have pen?' She asked.

It had been thirty-two years since I last saw my father. There had been few days in my childhood when I'd welcomed an audience with my Bageye. His titanic temper was bad enough, but the unpredictability was worse. What triggered the explosion was rarely possible to work out. Though its impact was more psychological terror than occasional physical pain, did I really want to revisit those times?

I had begun to write a memoir of my childhood, so arguably I had already made a start on the road back to the past. As the protagonist, whose name adorned the proposed title of the manuscript, *Bageye at the Wheel*, was still alive, I needed to get my childhood tormentor to sign off on it. You can't libel the dead, so perhaps I should have waited, but I doubted Bageye would have obliged by dying quickly enough.

Throughout my school years at St Columba's College in St Albans and beyond, my father had kept his distance. His small-time ganja dealing had funded my first year's school fees. I'd worked willingly and excitedly as his bag man, stashing the little home-made sachets of ganja in my briefcase, as he drove round Luton dropping off these little £5 bags of weed to all of his West Indian spars. I was never allowed into their houses. 'You mad?' No, I was instructed to wait in the car, with the engine running, as if I was his getaway driver. Not that Bageye ever seemed to be in a hurry. I never saw my father run. He was a man whose walk you couldn't copy; it was always just a bit off, just faster than slow.

Bageye's most impressive quality was reserved for the police, at which times he always showed a quick wit and lack of fear. There were plenty of reasons to be afraid, especially if stopped by police patrols when our car was laden with illicit goods, ganja or booze (knocked down in price, having been liberated from the local US military base in Lakenheath). But whenever we were flagged down by a constable, my father would step outside before required to and promote the policeman immediately. The bobby on the beat became 'Detective Inspector, Sir' or 'Chief Constable, Sir' – all said with a theatrical flair and an exaggeratedly respectful bow from Bageye. The PC would invariably be amused and end up waving us on with a gentle warning.

I was not so thrilled; it seemed embarrassing to see my father yet again subjugated in front of a white man. But when

I asked him what it all meant, he said, 'Sometimes you have to play fool fi ketch wise.'

It was a tricky strategy, but not as risky as breaking the law, I suppose. My father cast the trade in weed as a social service fulfilling a need – his spars had arrived in Britain with their love of ganja intact – rather than carrying out a criminal act. But when the police raided our house, following a tip-off, Bageye was arrested and the funds soon dried up. Though he never went to jail, our mother Ethlyn vowed never to cower before her husband ever again, and showed him the door.

Bageye couldn't believe his luck – sprung from the trap of a loveless marriage and ungrateful children. But he put on a show of being vexed before agreeing to depart, and he refused to surrender the keys to the house. I never understood why Ethlyn didn't change the lock on the front door.

In the following years, somehow my mother managed to keep me on at the expensive private school. When it came time to pay, at the end of each term, she and the bursar, Brother Raymond, danced around each other. Brother Raymond would send me home with a letter threatening my removal over missing school fees. I could guess the contents of the unopened letter from the sad, defeated gesture he made on handing it over, often followed by a tiny sigh. Ethlyn wouldn't even get to the end of Brother Raymond's letter before she reached for a pen and wrote back, asking the bursar to consider: what would Jesus do?

Bageye had never wavered in his determination to extinguish all traces of marriage and parenthood. In those lost years, though he was out of sight, I fantasised about him lurking in the vicinity and reappearing at significant moments. When, for instance, it was announced in the college's Great Hall that I was elected Head Boy, or the day the letter arrived announcing I'd been offered a place at the London Hospital Medical School,

'Praise God!' Ethlyn had dropped to her knees on such occasions, but no word ever came from Bageye.

During the decades of seeming indifference from my father, there were two things I most remembered about Bageye. The first was the sight of him doubled over in inexplicable abdominal pains that were only partially relieved by him drinking a chalky, milk-like substance. The pains were probably a manifestation of anxiety brought on by money and other worries. Secondly, there was his walk; defeated, but proud.

Digging around our family album, I found a fading black-and-white photo of a baby, cut out so that he appeared, with no background, only in outline. He seemed to be hovering in mid-air. That baby was me. In the original portrait, I was held up by Bageye. But a pair of scissors had been taken to the photo: he'd been excised. After our parents' separation, the man that my mother, my siblings and I called Satan was cut out of our lives and out of every photo.

I tried to conjure those photos as I made my way to the address given by Mrs Paulette. Bageye was now in his eighties and his flat was located in a 1970s block of sheltered accommodation, though he'd always protested that such an arrangement would never be his future. The block had an unimaginative, sleepy, institutional feel to it. The swing doors never swung back to properly close. It was early afternoon, yet the large, communal living room, with what seemed to be more than enough armchairs for every resident, was empty. I climbed the stairs towards the third-floor landing. Every step tested my conviction to continue. And then, eventually, there was no alternative other than to knock on the last remaining door at the end of the landing. I knocked, and immediately thought of running. There is always a point after which you know you can't turn back from a decision. The tension was in working out if you'd already reached that point. Through the frosted glass, I could see him approaching. A tiny, sprightly man opened the door. He held out his hand, and unthinkingly, surprisingly, I took it. We shook.

'Come in, come in; you're letting out all the heat,' he said. There was the beginning of a laugh in his voice, as he led me down the corridor. 'You turn big man, now!'

He wasn't wrong. I was barely a teenager on the last occasion I'd spoken to my father and we'd probably been the same height: five foot three. I was a foot taller than him now.

'So how Ethlyn?'

I was astonished by how casually he spoke.

'How your mother?'

I suppose you could say it was impressive – the impertinence of it. Bageye turned to look at me when I didn't answer. I couldn't look away from his familiar eyes, the bags deepening under them, with a second line, as it were, running beneath the first. At least the eyes were not aflame. In fact, they could have been described as lambent; Bageye was smiling. I had never known my father to smile. It was disconcerting.

There was a further surprise in the living room. Bageye had a friend with him – older than me, but not by much. I couldn't place him and Bageye pointedly failed to introduce the man who nodded but did not speak. This nameless friend had the formal air about him of a new arrivee from the old country, Jamaica probably. He was tall, taut and sinewy, slightly hunched over in a way that suggested, along with an old scar on his cheek, that he'd been a boxer. But, more than that, his stillness suggested menace, like a henchman or capo, or perhaps more of a consigliere like Robert Duvall's character in *The Godfather*. I hadn't stopped to think, until now, that Bageye might have been just as nervous of meeting me as I was of meeting him.

A number of specialist horse racing papers, opened on pages of lists of meetings, tips and odds, were strewn across a low coffee table – with the names of horses or jockeys marked with a cross beside them or underlined. Jockeyed horses raced across the TV screen. Even with the volume turned down, you could detect the calm commentary speeding up as they went through the furlongs. Bageye seemed torn between being attentive towards me – his special guest – and keeping an eye on the progress of his horse. He smiled as they crossed the finishing line and turned towards the consigliere holding up a finger. 'Bwoi, just one more, just – one – more!'

Apparently he needed one more win for the accumulator. Bageye tried to explain an accumulator to me and I feigned interest while trying to mask my surprise that my father was still gambling on that elusive big win despite a lifetime of losses. I imagine, like most gamblers, he was addicted to losing. During my childhood I recalled how he'd been unnerved by any substantial win and would quickly gamble away the winnings before being forced to change his losing streak.

There was no shape to our conversation. We just began, as if we were in a drama class and had been asked to improvise without so much as a prompt. I glanced around the room. There were few decorations. On the wall to my right a blue-eyed, haloed Jesus Christ put in an appearance. Above the portrait, a shelf was screwed to the wall. It had a solitary book on it: *Middlemarch* by George Eliot.

'What did you make of *Middlemarch*?' I asked. Bageye looked perplexed, so I pointed at the shelf.

Bageye smiled. 'It don't finish.'

My father seemed to have only the most tentative claim on the flat. I knew that if I ever opened the kitchen drawer that there'd only be a couple of knives, forks and spoons in it. It wasn't just sparse; it was perfunctory, as if Bageye was camping in the flat, or as if he'd just moved in temporarily, had received basic furnishings from a charity shop and was holding out for something better.

'How long have you lived here?' I asked.

'Quite a while now.'

'On your own? Just you one?' I asked, slipping back into, mirroring, the way my father spoke.

'Why you aks?'

'Just asking?'

'You aks without a reason?' Bageye turned to his consigliere. 'A man who aks without a reason, there's a reason why he aks.'

'True dat,' answered the consigliere.

'Just me one,' said Bageye, with the finality of a gambler playing a trump card, killing any further line of questioning. 'I man alone.'

'I was just asking.'

'You want to go round once more?'

My father had the ability to look aggrieved and apologetic at the same time. He seemed to seek assurance from his consigliere who, I now recognised, served more as a cornerman or one of those church elders stationed on the platform beside the pastor, punctuating his sermons with 'amen', 'that's right' and 'yes, Lord'.

They exchanged some 'old-time talk'. Bageye beamed, and leaned in, telling his friend proudly as he pointed to me: 'This boy and me go back, you know; have a deep, deep connection.'

The consigliere nodded sagely, 'Aye sah, that's no jacket.'

A 'jacket', I knew, was a bastard child, so what the consigliere had said was meant as a compliment.

'A deep, deep connection,' repeated Bageye, 'Nah true?'

The pulse of that connection might have been beating

strongly in Bageye but I did not feel it; if there was a pulse, it was weak and hardly registered. Truthfully, it was more of a delicate thread than a rope that bound us. He kept glancing over to me as if he feared I might disappear just as miraculously as I'd arrived. And I had the peculiar feeling that I was somehow disappointing him by my coolness.

'What took you?'

'Usual hold-ups on the M25. Sorry.'

'No, I mean what took you?'

'What do you mean?'

'You know what I mean.'

'Oh you mean the thirty . . . what is it – thirty-two years?'

'You aksing me? Is me you aks?'

Bageye's voice snapped like a flag in the wind. It was a reflex. He looked hurt and disappointed.

'Remember that time, you saw me in the Arndale Centre,' he accused, 'and you turned around and walked away?'

'Really? I don't think so. When was this?'

'Ten, twelve year ago.'

'I don't think so. No. You're mistaken.'

'I'm not mistaken. It was you, all right. It was you!' He smiled but not in a pleasant manner and I calculated in just how many ways it had been foolish to come looking for him.

My father was always a difficult man to read. In a continual foul mood that was never ameliorated, in our presence at least, and possessing an unnerving combustibility, forever asking, 'who left the lid of the toilet seat up?' or 'who left the toilet seat down?' (confusingly both were wrong things to have done), he resembled the grumbling, cursing cartoon character Yosemite Sam. I could see, whenever I accompanied him, to lime with his spars, though, that Bageye was temperamentally closer to the mischievous 'What's up Doc?' cunning of Yosemite Sam's infuriating carrot-chomping nemesis. There was no shiver of regret from him now, only the copper-plated certainty that I, his ungrateful pickney, had neglected him, and not the other way round.

'Well, your reality is your reality,' I said. 'Let's not have an atmosphere.' I reached into my bag. 'I've brought you a present.'

I carefully arranged, as I'd practised before setting out for Luton, two of my books, placing them on top of the latest work, a ring-bound new manuscript. I handed the little bundle to him. Bageye held them briefly before passing the bundle to the consigliere. His action, too, looked rehearsed, as if he'd been expecting them all along.

'Your brother, Milton. Him bring him pickney see me.' Bageye paused to lick the sticky side of a cigarette paper, finishing off what he'd started before I'd rung the doorbell. 'You bring me books.'

'But that a peace offering, right there, sah,' said the consigliere.

'The man kind. Oh yes,' Bageye laughed. 'Him kind, all right!'

'Maybe too kind?'

Bageye laughed. So, too, did the consigliere. But when I joined in, my father snapped: 'What do you want?'

'Excuse me, but what do you mean by "Milton?"' I asked.

'What?'

'You said Milton bring his pickney see you. Milton came here?'

'Yes.'

'Why would he come?'

'Why wouldn't he come? I'm the bwoi father. See him there.' Bageye gestured over my shoulder.

Behind me, hung on the wall, was a framed studio photo – a lifeless, soft-focus, portrait of Milton, my elder brother, his wife and child. The consigliere stood to inspect the photo.

'I'm the boy father,' Bageye repeated slowly. 'The pickney grandfather. I have a jar for she. See it there.'

He pointed to a jar full of coins. 'Only £2 coins Popsie say me must give her.'

'It heavy.' The consigliere nodded approvingly as he picked up the big jar. 'It have whole 'eap.'

'She come and take it away. I must fill it up whenever Milton bring her come.' Bageye reached into his trouser pocket for another coin and as the consigliere unscrewed the top, Bageye dropped it into the jar.

'Nice, nice,' said the consigliere.

Nice? For a moment I contemplated pushing a fist into my father's face, pounding it until it was a bloody mess. 'How many times? How many times has Milton come?' I asked. But if Bageye heard he wasn't answering. For decades, my siblings and I had kept to an unspoken pact to shun Satan. We all knew what he was; you couldn't escape that fact. I'd only contacted the devil out of necessity and with the blessing of all the siblings, including Milton. My brother didn't mention that he'd already opened up a line of communication with the enemy.

Bageye stood, unbruised, and, without lighting his cigarette, made his way to the bathroom. Now that I was alone with the consigliere I thought he might volunteer some basic information, but we both sat in enforced, self-conscious quiet, trying not to listen to the sound of Bageye's urine hitting the basin of the toilet. Eventually I surrendered, as I knew I must and asked, 'So how do you know Clinton?'

'That man has done great things,' answered the consigliere. 'He is a man who has done great things.'

I wondered what kind of great things he had in mind, but the consigliere said they were too many to mention. In that moment I realised, with absolute certainty, that I was in the presence of one of Bageye's relatives. And in fact, looking more closely now, it was obvious that the consigliere wasn't older but younger than me; his old-fashioned clothes had confused me.

'Sorry, I didn't catch your name.'

'Country.'

'Country? Oh so you're Country. Funny, someone said we sound alike.'

'You lie!'

'No, it's true.'

'You joke.'

'Just the other day. And I remember thinking it was very odd, not odd, just unusual, the name . . . I mean. How did you get the name?'

Country didn't seem impressed by the question. He looked at me as if I'd just stepped in shit and was showing him the underside of my shoe.

'I mean, I'm not trying to chat your business or anything,' I said. 'I'm just curious.'

Back in the bathroom the peeing paused, and Bageye shouted, 'Him name Country 'cause him is a Country bwoi!'

'Country man!' the consigliere corrected. They both spluttered with laughter and Bageye's peeing recommenced.

When he returned to the living room, I asked more sharply than I intended whether he had replaced the toilet seat. 'The lid of the toilet seat. Did you leave it up or put it down?'

Bageye chuckled, 'You aks too many question.'

'Well did you? Leave it up or put it down?'

'What kinda foolishness this? Who care?'

'You care.'

'Cho man!'

'You care! You care – a lot. Don't you remember? You care a hell of a lot.'

I got up and went to inspect the toilet and position of the seat, even though I'd worked out as an adult, looking back on my childhood, that the man's rage had little to do with the position of the blasted seat. 'It's down. Oh my God, it's down!' I said as I re-entered the room and slumped into my armchair. I felt the air leave my lungs and not return. The room was suffocating; the armchair paralysing. It was impossible to move. 'Breathe, just inhale,' I told myself, 'then exhale. In. Out. In. Out.'

No one spoke, or even seemed inclined to, for quite a while. It was a relief when Bageye's mobile phone eventually rang. He half turned in his chair and whispered into the mouthpiece but loud enough, inadvertently, for me to hear, 'He's here now.' Bageye cursed when, having switched off the phone, it rang accusingly once more. He fumbled all fingers and thumbs, powered it off, considered ringing back but decided against it after all.

'Who was that?'

'Friend,' answered Bageye.

I didn't push him further. Instead, I took a chance and apologised. What was I apologising for? He wanted to know. I wasn't sure, but asked if we could start again, if we could reset the conversation and the reunion.

My father flashed a diamond smile at Country and pointing to me said, 'That my spar, right there, sah. Me nah tell you?'

Bageye and his new-found spar agreed to go to The Chequers for a late pub lunch; Country would remain in the flat as, he said, he didn't want to spoil the party. But he risked spoiling our departure in an awkward exchange with Bageye who was attempting to borrow some cash from Country that had already been handed over just an hour previously, apparently.

'You forget?'

'I don't forget when it come to money,' answered Bageye.

'What about the breast pocket?'

'I have wallet,' Bageye fixed Country with his fury. 'When a man have wallet, what sense him put him money in a breast pocket?'

'Well what's that?' Country indicated a £20 note sticking out at the top of the breast pocket of Bageye's crisply ironed shirt.

'Who put that there? I don't know how it get there. I don't!'

'Must be ghost.'

Bageye backed out of the argument and into his bedroom to select a hat of the day; he'd a range of a dozen to choose from.

'This could take a while,' mumbled Country, not particularly to me. He was right. When Bageye finally emerged, he was dressed to a point beyond distinction with razor-sharp creased trousers and spats. He'd chosen a fedora and also sported a fine walking stick with an elegant silver handle. Before we could leave, though, he just wanted to settle a little business with Country. But even before Bageye opened his mouth, Country reminded him that the £20 note was in his breast pocket.

My father checked his breast pocket and his face beheld a miracle. 'Just a borrows,' he assured Country, transferring the £20 to his wallet as we moved towards the front door. Bageye told me to go ahead. He said he couldn't manage the stairs and so would take the chair lift down.

Far from being embarrassed, he looked delighted with the thrill of descending on the chair lift. As I waited for him at the bottom, it was hard to reckon the vision of this amiable dandyish older gent gliding towards me, with the memory of the man who'd once pushed my mother down the stairs and broken her leg.

Still, there was the matter of the manuscript to attend to. We'd barely spoken about it, but I clocked now that Bageye held it firmly in his grip, as we walked towards the pub. I struggled, adjusting my steps, to match his slowness, which somehow felt more wilful on his part than necessary. Of course, my father had his signature walk, and nothing, not even a reunion with a long-lost son, was going to make him change his stride.

The Chequers was a bleak-looking place with outside boards over the windows more usually associated with strip clubs. It turned out that its windows had been smashed and were awaiting repair. The pub's dark interior and basic furniture favoured hard-drinking patrons whose focus was on the pints not the aesthetics; not a strip club then but, aside from Mrs Paulette, in the absence of other women, it appeared to be a 'bull pen'.

Pushing through the door of the saloon bar, the regulars called out Bageye's name in a welcome that might have signalled his popularity more successfully had it not seemed so rehearsed. Underlying the staginess, an affable Rasta – well, at least one whose oversized cap housing his locks suggested the accoutrements of the religion – shouted for all the old-timers and especially Bageye to hear, 'The prodigal son return!' He kind of skipped across in a strange chorea, like a swimmer ducking under and then breaking the surface of the sea, to pat me on the back. He pretended injury when I failed to recognise him. I should not have been surprised to learn the nickname of this fidgety man: Be Still. He must have been taking a sabbatical from his Rasta tenets, as draining the dregs of his Guinness, Be Still held out his empty glass and asked, 'So Bageye wha'appen, we gwan toast the son return?'

Bageye kissed his teeth and addressed Mrs Paulette over the counter of the bar. 'How many time? Is how many time I must tell this man?' He turned to face Be Still and said very slowly, enunciating each word, 'I. Don't. Business. With. You.' This, too, felt performative, like sport, especially when Be Still followed us over to the table Mrs Paulette had reserved for us and planted his backside down on one of the stools.

'What you drinking?' asked Be Still.

'You don't know by now?'

'What about the boy?'

'See him there.'

I resisted the default temptation to order a soft drink and suggested a craft beer. Bageye answered Be Still's bemusement with, 'Get him the same as me.' He surrendered the only note in his wallet to Be Still who only got up from his stool once Bageye added, 'and one for yourself.'

'Great waiter service they have here,' I whispered.

'Never kick a man when he's down,' Bageye spoke gravely. 'He gwan get up and kick you back. My father never teach me to be a rogue. A rogue I shall not be.'

It was the first time I'd ever heard him mention his father. In fact, now that I reflected on it, it was the first time he'd ever talked about any of his family. I thought I detected a tear in Bageye's eye but could not locate any accompanying emotion in his face. I was not yet ready to complicate my disdain for the man, as he would discover when he read the manuscript I'd brought with me. And with uncanny purpose, as if he lived in the realm of my senses, Bageye now turned to that very document. He smiled at the picture of himself – forty years younger – which graced the cover. He shot out of his seat and held up the manuscript towards the men assembled at the bar. He kept the book aloft until he had the bar's full attention and beamed:

'My son a-write book 'pon me!'

I should not have underestimated the vanity of the man.

'A book! You don't hear?' He continued amidst the uproar with some of the men laughing and others cheering.

'My son has written a book, book you know, a book, about me!' The excitement rose, pure excitement. Be Still returned, astonishingly balancing three glasses of whisky in one hand. Other men left their drinks behind and gathered round.

'A book?' Asked one of the men. 'But what Bageye know 'bout book?'

'Him have headucation,' Be Still countered. There was much guffawing. Although the ribbing was good-natured, I felt drawn to Bageye's defence.

'This man has done great things,' I said.

'A who dis? Him talk like Henglishman.'

Viewing the photo of Bageye on the front page of the manuscript, someone asked: 'Why him look so vex?'

'Stop your noise!' Bageye shouted back at him.

'You don't have no better picture?'

'Him face favour bull, eeh!'

The eruption of chat – teasing and provocation – was nonstop. Mrs Paulette must have witnessed my bewilderment. 'Don't pay them no mind,' she spoke above the hubbub, 'all-a dem like batty and chamber.' The applause and commotion was dribbling away, the bar returning to its sleepy rhythm, when two young women, in their late 20s, early 30s, walked in. Bageye beckoned them and they made their way to our table, accompanied by the smooth sound of their satin skirts as they sashayed over. I stood up, much to Bageye's amusement.

'Is my son, dat,' he said, introducing me to the two women, Mel and Shirley.

'Oh, what lovely manners,' said Mel.

Be Still took a chance to further ingratiate himself with Bageye. 'He tek after the father.'

'Nah, the bwoi go private school,' Bageye explained. 'A-wha' you expect? A little bit of polish.'

Shirley cooed, 'So you go posh school?'

'That's right.'

'You is the doctor, right?'

'Not anymore.'

'Him writer now. See.' Bageye passed the manuscript to Mel. 'Bestseller. All like J. K. Rowling and t'ing.'

Mel flicked to the end. 'TBC?'

'To be continued. It's not finished.'

'Oh.'

'A work-in-progress,' I explained.

'How does it end then?'

'It end,' Bageye jumped in, 'when him write "The End". Right, my friend?' Bageye took back the manuscript and handed it to me. 'You gwan sign it?'

He suggested I sign it 'To Pops' but that was a step too far. I felt the heat of his gaze as I hesitated before scribbling: 'To my father'.

Bageye nodded, 'That's fair. Couldn't ask for more. That's fair.'

'Fadder and son!' said Be Still. 'Prodigal son return!'

Paulette announced that the kitchen would be closed in five minutes, prompting Bageye to ask of Be Still: 'Any change leave?'

'Paulette keep it . . . from last time,' he said sheepishly. 'She say you still owe from last time.'

'A wha' dis? Don't start talk tripe in my ear hole.' Bageye leaned over to me. 'You hungry? You like chicken?'

'Mmmh, I'm vegetarian.'

'Good,' said Bageye. 'If you see what fowl eat you never eat meat'. He winked at Mel and Shirley before shouting to Mrs Paulette for two plates of jerk chicken with rice 'n' peas – 'Breast now, not one of them dead-for-nothing scrawny leg or wing.' One plate was for his son, he told her, and he'd come back for the other.

My father winked at me as Mrs Paulette sashayed back to the bar, a loyal soldier in the army of Bageye, carrying out her commander's order. I was suddenly overcome with a feeling of warmth, being among all of these Caribbean people. I loved the mischief of their talk and the overall barbed bonhomie. So what if I'd only tracked down the old man to ensure that he didn't cause trouble when the book came out? So what if it transpired that Country was actually his son from another woman and family that we'd always suspected Bageye of having? This was a moment, right? Just enjoy it, right? Right.

'Why couldn't we be like this before?' I said.

'Like what?'

'You know, hanging out, liming, talking shit.'

'Well, me still have teet' in my head,' said Bageye. 'Me not gwan anywhere. You find me now. Find me again. Simple so.'

Easy, perhaps. But I knew instinctively that I would not return.

'Yes man, you have my number? Wheel and come again.'

And with that, he stood up with Mel and Shirley, thrust his hands into the pockets of his jacket, and extended his elbows so that the women could thread their arms through his. Together, all three now linked arm-in-arm, prepared to walk out of The Chequers.

'What's going on?' I asked.

'Time to go.'

'Where to . . . where are you going?'

'Oh, these are my bookies,' Bageye said of the women, walking to the door of the saloon bar. 'Me win 'pon the accumulator. We gwan to the office.'

Before they left, Bageye whispered something to Mrs Paulette. The landlady disappeared into the kitchen, I suppose, and then came back out, sashaying towards me, balancing a tray. She placed a plate of chicken wings and rice on the table. I must have looked perplexed.

'Breast finish,' she said.

A huge picture of a ram took up most of the front page of the *Luton News*. Underneath was an account of an unusual criminal heist: some rare and expensive rams had been abducted from a farm at a nearby village. The headline joked, 'Can Ewe Believe It?' Halfway down the column on the right-hand side of the paper there was a passport-sized photo of Bageye, with the promise of a news story about him on page 4.

Months after my meeting with Bageye, the *Luton News*, having heard about the reunion, got in touch and asked for an interview. Forget the *Guardian*, *Telegraph* or the *Sun*; for decades, the *Luton News* had served as the paper of record and of choice for local people. How could I say, no?

When asked about my motivation for the reunion, I told the reporter, Bev, that my last real connection with Bageye had been as an eleven-year-old boy – and having an eleven-year-old son myself now had made me think about Bageye with much more compassion. The meeting had been surprisingly good-natured.

'And what was Dad like, after all these years?' asked Bev. I described my father – 'Not Dad,' I corrected the journalist, 'God, no' – as a twinkly eyed eighty-three-year-old chap who still had an eye for the ladies (his bookies) and they for him. I also included some local colour about my love of Luton. To my eyes, as a ten-year-old looking down on the shimmering lights of the town from the Farley Hill estate, it could have been Las Vegas, a fantastic metropolis.

Another month or so passed before the article was supposed to come out and when it was imminent, I alerted Bageye about it. By now almost a year had passed since I'd handed him the manuscript. Then I rang my father on the day when the feature, with the headline, 'Autobiography which could heal a three-decade rift for Farley Hill family', was published in the *Luton News*. Bageye answered on his mobile phone, in the street. He was extremely agitated. It wasn't just the result of his emphysema from a lifelong relationship with tobacco; he sounded as if he was hyperventilating.

'How dare you write those things about me?'

'What things?'

'You know what things?'

'I really don't. What are you talking about?'

'If you want jackass for ride, here comes Bageye?'

The article had vexed him, it seemed, so much so that he'd picked up the manuscript, and reading it now, perhaps for the first time, he'd found things he didn't like. Ethlyn had never had a kind word to say about her husband. 'He wasn't even a good gambler,' was her constant refrain. 'The other man them, the poker player, lick them chops when they see him. Time evening end, the fool would have lost everything, nah mus', 'cause if you want to ride a jackass Bageye your man.'

'That was just an amusing aside, c'mon,' I pleaded. 'It's what Ethlyn used to say all the time.'

'Amusing? You're telling the whole world you think your father's a jackass.'

'Wait a second.'

79

'I don't have time for this,' Bageye paused before continuing, 'I'm on my way to see my solicitor.'

The phone went dead and he didn't pick up when I tried calling him back.

I rang again and this time, he picked up but didn't speak.

Bageye wasn't saying a word, not one word. I could hear him wheezing, though, struggling to breathe. I pleaded with the old man to read the article and the manuscript with an unprejudiced eye. 'Give it time.' I asked him not to do anything too rash. Finally, I suggested that I should jump into my car and come to see him. From Brighton to Luton was just a couple of hours up the motorway. I'd come in the evening. It was only after I'd been speaking for a while that I realised that Bageye had once more turned off his phone.

I suppose there wasn't a better time for self-reflection and now that I thought about it, I conceded 'If you want jackass for ride, here comes Bageye,' wasn't too flattering.

Before I could get on the road to Luton, I had to negotiate with two of the most formidable people I know: my sister, Shirley, and my mother Ethlyn. Both women, whom Jamaicans would have called 'tallawah' (small, but mighty), lived together down the road from where I now lived in Brighton, and insisted on coming with me back to our hometown. Neither of them had seen Bageye for thirty years and, though they didn't relish the encounter, they feared, they said, that I was too pliant for the 'evil wretch'; that my 'too refined' constitution was ill-prepared for argument, and that I was a smart but 'educated fool' who was voluntarily entering enemy territory. I needed back-up, they suggested; they'd ride shotgun. I refused their offers, put on my coat, said goodbye, took a few deep breaths, opened the front door and headed out. Before I reached my car, I heard my sister and eighty-year-old mother hurrying out of the house. They reached the car ahead of me and stood beside it, arms crossed and defiant. I was already nervous about the possibility of fireworks when I returned to Luton; now they were guaranteed.

The motorway was busy, but we were all silent in the car, alone with our thoughts and strategies, perhaps. Ethlyn seemed especially tense. Her sighs were punctuated with occasional, explosive outbursts that seemed to come from the past – 'Satan! I'm not in the mood for you today, Satan.' – talking to herself, but really talking to Bageye. Growing up with her in the 1960s and 70s, I recalled her past dislike of argument 'I can't stand the contention,' she'd berate us children whenever a squabble arose, though she would never back away from a fight. Watching her and Bageye tear into each other over the years was like having a ringside seat at a heavyweight boxing match with merciless sluggers who failed to deliver the knockout blow; it was never ending and attritional. More often than not Bageye would up sticks and retire, leaving the house, bruised and furious, slamming the front door behind him.

I'd grown up mindful of the memory of those confrontations and taken on the role of the family's peacekeeper. How odd, then, to have invited conflict through writing about the past. We pulled off the motorway and headed towards the town. 'Mum, I think it's best that you don't come into the flat,' I said.

'I'm not staying in the car.'

I suggested that I drive to a local Pizza Express, close to the flat, and drop her off there. 'You have your phone, right? We'll text if there's any trouble.'

'I don't have my glasses.'

'Phone then, we'll phone. Right, Shirley?'

Shirley agreed, but Ethlyn shook her head, 'My bad eye a-dance.' When she was nervous her right eye twitched or 'danced', she'd say, a sign she thought ominous, though I had suggested it simply signalled a need for more calcium in her diet.

'My bad eye a-dance,' she warned. 'I see trouble . . . I see trouble. You know how that man stay. Blood mus' follow vein.'

Only when I threatened to turn the car around and head back onto the motorway and back to Brighton did she relent. I said we'd 'soon come' for her and meant it; I had no intention of staying a second longer than was needed.

Outside of the block of flats, I thought of establishing a few ground rules with Shirley. 'Let me do the talking, OK?'

'I didn't come all this way just to hold my tongue,' she answered.

I had always admired Shirley's fearlessness and directness; even at rest she seemed to wear an invisible protective exoskeleton, charged with a high voltage that was dangerous to touch.

'If anything, I think it's best you let me do the talking.' Shirley spoke with the kind of judicial certainty of a well-briefed barrister, addressing her client in the hall leading to the courtroom.

I knocked firmly on the door to Bageye's flat. He opened the door with magnificent, righteous fury but flinched at the sight of Shirley. His daughter was a rabbit punch he hadn't anticipated.

'Oh is you, Shirley. Never thought you would ever a-come.' Bageye actually sounded grateful.

'Good to see you, too,' said Shirley. She was courteous and cool. We all stepped into the living room. As before, Country was there, sitting in the same chair, giving the impression that he hadn't moved from the previous occasion. He stood to acknowledge Shirley and smiled, despite himself.

Shirley held forth. She explained that she was only here in

Bageye's flat because of her mother and brother. She carried no brief for past hurts, she said. This was not a position she had ever dreamed of finding herself in, and she did not want any tea, water, tobacco, ganja or any damn thing Bageye might be tempted to offer. She didn't see the point of false courtesies but we could at least refrain from verbal abuse. Ultimately, Shirley suggested, she was only here to 'stop the contention'.

'I'm not signing anything,' said Bageye.

'We haven't brought anything to sign,' Shirley answered. 'Why would you say that?'

'Well, I'm not signing anything.' Bageye looked to Country, for confirmation.

'He's not signing anything,' said Country.

'What's it got to do with you?' I barked, and immediately regretted my tone.

'My solicitor has advised . . .'

'Solicitor?' asked Shirley. 'So, what's your complaint?'

Bageye took a clean handkerchief from his pocket and used it to dab away the eye-water (not tears) that had collected on the bottom lid of his right eye. 'He's telling the whole world that he thinks his father is a jackass! "If you want jackass for ride, here comes Bageye."'

'Is that it?' asked Shirley. 'So, you'd like that line removed, deleted?'

'And a sheep rustler!'

Both Shirley and I were perplexed by the sheep-rustler remark. By way of explanation, Bageye picked up the *Luton News* and held it out, as if to members of the jury, with its front-page picture of the rare rams. It dawned on me that Bageye had conflated the *Luton News* story with an amusing (I thought) story that I'd included in the manuscript. It was the tale of Joe Barnes, a long-distance lorry-driving friend of

Bageye's, who'd fallen out with him and who had kidnapped a sheep from a farm one day and brought it to our house as a peace offering (once butchered, it would have provided food for the winter). By a strange and unbelievable coincidence the *Luton News* had a similar-sounding story on its front page.

'I've never been a sheep rustler!'

'But that was Joe Barnes,' I countered. 'And it was just an amusing anecdote. You read the book?'

'Enough.'

'How about you?' I asked Country.

'Yes, it was funny. The truth is, you should have written it as a novel.'

'OK. OK.' Shirley had heard enough. She turned and spoke directly to Bageye. 'So what do you want?'

'I'm not signing anything,' Bageye repeated. 'My solicitor says not to sign.'

'I see.' Shirley, seeing Bageye's growing agitation and breathlessness, suggested that he sit down. Bageye refused.

'All right then,' said Shirley, 'so it sounds like you want to embark on some kind of litigious path. By all means, take Colin to court. At court, the judge will ask: well is any of this that Colin has written true? You will say, no, it's all a pack of lies. But all his siblings and Ethlyn will answer that it's all true.'

'Me and your mother never get on,' Bageye countered.

But Shirley wasn't finished. She said that the court would hear that not only was it all true, but that I had diluted the truth. Shirley then proceeded to list a catalogue of violence that I had decided not to include in the manuscript. She started with the incident of Bageye pushing Ethlyn down the stairs. Bageye winced at the memory. Then there was the time he broke a flowerpot over her head, and the boiling water that he had thrown at her.

With each of Shirley's evidential recollections, Bageye took a step back, reeling, as if he were trying to back out of the conversation and out of the memory. His look of astonishment was matched by Country's incomprehension and embarrassment.

'And then there was the time,' Shirley continued, 'when Ethlyn was at the ironing board and you wrestled the iron from her hand and tried to push it into her face.' Bageye groaned and left the room. We heard the tap running in the kitchen.

Country shouted over, asking if he was all right and whether he needed oxygen. It was only then that I noticed an oxygen tank by the far window. Bageye returned a minute later. He stood to attention as a defendant might, awaiting the jury's verdict.

'Me and your mother never get on,' he repeated meekly. Our father determinedly looked away from Shirley and me, but was also suddenly shy of Country, it seemed. 'Me will have to see what the solicitor say,' Bageye nodded to himself by way of agreement. 'But, I wouldn't want to do anything to damage the book,' he added.

His earlier battle-ready spikiness having drained away, he walked defeatedly to the front door and held it open for us. 'Tell Ethlyn hello from me,' he said, as we passed through the hallway, out of his flat and once more out of his life.

Before the *Luton News*'s intervention I had begun to think of Bageye in a more generous light, to consider the possibility of talking with him, without rancour; to imagine having the kind of conversations with him that I wished we'd had when I was a child. It was not to be. Days after the truce, my father marched to the HQ of the *Luton News* and demanded a right of reply. He got it with the headline: 'Bageye Bites Back'.

In a way, I admired him. In his eyes, I imagined, Bageye had held to his code. Whether there was any truth or substance to my account, he was not going to allow his colours to be dragged through the mud. What would he have achieved if it meant that we went back to another thirty years of silence? Bageye was a 'simple sense man'. I suppose he'd have shrugged and said, 'Well if it so, then it so.'

In any event, the affair died down; there was no more communication. But then one afternoon, my mobile phone rang. It was Bageye.

'Hello, how are you?' I asked.

'Country?'

'No, it's Creg.'

'Is Country that?'

I sensed what had happened. In his phone directory Country must have come just after Colin; he had called me by mistake.

'No, it's your son.'

'Not Country?'

'It's your son, Colin.'

'Oh, I see.'

The phone was shut off abruptly. That was that. It was fair enough. I recalled my own phone call to The Chequers more than a year earlier. Perhaps it had all been too soon, for both of us, after all. No matter how long I stared at it, the phone did not come back to life.

Herman

Today fi me, tomorrow fi you

What do you do when your father, whom you've built up as a monster, turns out to have been a straw man, a fragile figure, a candidate for compassion, a terroriser who subsequently appears to be – how can I say this delicately – pathetic? The best approach, surely, is to dig in and revert to thinking of him as an undeserving dog, an ogre; to hold onto your decades-old flame of resentment.

But there was no getting around the fact that the beanie man who'd loomed so long in my imagination as a giant, was something of a disappointment. Unfairly, I'd come to see other West Indian men of Bageye's generation in a similar vein. They'd all been giants in my childhood. When slighted by the English, they turned up the collars of their coats and walked on. When the favourite racehorse they'd bet their shirt on failed even to place, they didn't blink. Such style! But where was all that dignity now? Where had all the dreams gone of the zoot-suited saga boys who strode down the gangway of the Empire *Windrush* and the many other ships?

'Rahted' man, why, after venturing 4,000 miles from their cinnamon-scented islands, had these pioneers settled for a regular seat at a West Indian pub with Guinness on tap; for endlessly hanging out at Ladbrokes' or Coral's? They were shipwrecked men, as lost as Doc Saunders. But the saddest, who'd most tragically departed from the script, were those about whom Ethlyn would have shaken her head and said, 'England mad them.'

Mile End Road, coming to an abrupt stop at the intersection of Cambridge Heath and Whitechapel, is so called because it's exactly a mile from the City of London. I know this because Herman Harcourt told me so. But then in the same breath, he also said that he'd more than once walked the entire length of Mile End Road heel-to-toe and that it had seasonal variations, contracting seven feet in the winter. For weeks he'd been alarmed about the shortening, worried that maybe his feet were still growing, before arriving at this welcome revelation. Herman considered himself something of an amateur anthropologist of the East End, but he wasn't always a reliable witness, on account of his condition.

A not-so-contestable fact is that in London's rush hour you'll find at least one schizophrenic on every double-decker bus – that is statistically 1:100. This was one of the first things we learned in medical school in 1981. This, along with our tutor's mantra that there was pathology all around us, and that we should pay close attention – 'Think pathology; always be thinking pathology!' But once you arrive at that way of thinking, is there any way back? Although I didn't frame the question that way at the time, a version of it haunted me throughout my first year as I made my way along Mile End Road to Whitechapel each day, either on foot, bus or by bicycle, from my shared house in Bow.

There was plenty of pathology on view – TB, bronchitis, tertiary syphilis and myriad mental illnesses. Of all the schizophrenics who joined the number 25 bus on that short stretch during rush hour, Herman Harcourt was the most frequent.

The first time I came across Herman there was something familiar about him. Exiting from Whitechapel Station, I heard a loud and distinctive speaky-spokey, West Indian voice. As we squeezed past the ticket collector's box and spilled out onto the pavement, above the sing-song tirade of stallholders, discounting fruit and veg, offering 'Pound o' bananas fifty. Pound o' bananas fifty,' you could just make out that singularly Caribbean accent in the distance, shouting what sounded like 'Knee grows occurs.'

His words were high-pitched; the man appeared to be hyperventilating. The gaps between his shrieks shortened until they merged into a prolonged awful-sounding howl. At the same time, all along the pavement, one cluster after another, the pedestrians began to part. Someone or something was coming and could not be stopped. People peeled away as if instructed. It all seemed bizarre; as surreally choreographed as those feathered showgirls on television in the black-and-white musicals I'd sat through on Saturday evenings, raising their plumes in sequence to reveal, finally, the tap-dancing stars in dinner jacket and sequined evening dress.

This particular Fred Astaire turned out to be Herman Harcourt. He thrust through the mass of people on that sweltering afternoon, wrapped in a heavy overcoat with a piece of cord pulled tightly around his waist and emerged just as I knew he would, in line with the onset of déjà vu, that elusive and uncanny feeling of events unfolding marginally ahead of your memory of them.

He was no more than fifty, but old enough to have been my father, and was obviously on the run, perhaps from a shopkeeper. In each hand he gripped numerous bulging plastic bags; they formed a ring around him as encumbering as any Victorian lady's layer of petticoats and his voice became increasingly strident and urgent until what he was actually screaming became clear: 'Negroes are cursed!'

This strange bag man was bearing down on me, and I could move neither left nor right, backwards nor forwards. I was gripped by a paralysis and a collision seemed inevitable. But somehow, with his plastic bags flapping at his side, Herman brushed past, so close there could not have been a piece of tissue paper between us; so close I caught a whiff of the fug of sweat and tobacco on his dirty overcoat. He easily outpaced his pursuers, a man and woman in their forties. If he'd continued, he might have gotten away, but he suddenly stopped and began walking backwards, retracing his steps precisely and nervously, as if in a minefield. When he reached me, he put down his bags, bent over and picked up a cigarette butt, pinched it back into shape and shoved it into his coat pocket. That's when they caught up and pounced. Not in a rough way; more like anxious parents who had lost their child in the crowd. I've often wondered why Herman stopped. It seemed such an odd thing to do. Everything might have turned out differently had he kept on going.

'Don't let them take me,' Herman pleaded. 'Please! They're impostors. Don't let them take me!'

By now the man had put Herman Harcourt in an armlock. 'Do not be alarmed, he is harmless really,' he said. 'No need for alarm, is there Herman?'

'Ah who you a-call Herman?'

'I am just saying that you are harmless, are you not? I am paying you a compliment, Herman.'

'Listen how the man call my name. Is so you call me name, in the street? In the street?!'

'Now Herman,' pleaded the man.

'I know you?'

'Hermaaaan, pleeaasse.'

In the absence of anyone else foolish enough to slow down

and pay attention to what was going on, Herman turned and confided to me: 'Me nah know the man, you know.' He scrutinised his captor, searching for clues, until he found that which confirmed his suspicions. 'Look at his feet. Him an impostor. Didn't I tell you? Him an impostor, man. Just look at his feet. You see any sock on the man feet?'

Though the man wore sensible black patent-leather shoes, Herman Harcourt was agitated and exercised over his absence of socks. I confess that I too thought it curious.

'But Herman, you are not wearing socks either,' said the man.

The news hit Herman hard. He trembled. Seconds passed, perhaps a minute before he steadied himself and was brave enough to look down: 'Oh Lord, dem gone with me socks!'

Herman's anguish was pitiful, but the man seemed amused by the direction the conversation had taken. His laughing lips were held in check only by the vexed gaze of his colleague, who had a professional tenderness about her and a countenance more in keeping with a chaperone.

The setback with the socks was enough to remind Herman – how could he have forgotten? – that 'Negroes are cursed!' He repeated this endlessly, as if gamely trying a tongue-twister. 'Negroes are cursed! Negroes are cursed!' He broke free from the man's grip. He turned and turned, not moving from the spot, like a child trying to make himself dizzy. Finally, he slumped. He couldn't raise his suddenly heavy head; his chin rested on his chest.

The minders propped him up like cornermen to a boxer at the end of a bruising round. After some adjustment of positions (the choreography appeared to have been thought through), all three were ready to move off, not quite arm-in-arm, but linked to such a degree that if one moved the others were bound to follow. Before they reached the corner, Herman turned back towards me. Would they allow him a word of advice to the young man? He didn't wait for permission, but shuffled in my direction. His chaperones, loosening but not releasing their grip, snaked along with him.

'In private – a word in private, if you please,' he whispered.

The woman straightened the collar of Herman's overcoat and smoothed the lapel with the back of her hand. 'No more secrets. Remember? Who said that? Did you say it and not mean it? Was that you being insincere?'

Herman shook his head vigorously.

'Good. So what is it you want to say?'

'All I wanted to say to the young man . . .' Herman began graciously, but almost immediately his tone hardened, 'because he looks like a decent young man, although looks can be deceiving. I wanted him to know, looking all smug and pleased with himself . . .' He paused to jab a finger at me. 'Brutus. *Et tu, Brutus*? I come not to praise him. He knows what he's done. But I want to offer a word of advice, my friend. If they come for me in the morning, they'll be coming for you in the afternoon.'

The chaperone squirmed as she tried to fashion some kind of apology. I thought to lessen her discomfort by saying to Herman that I had no idea what he was talking about. Except I'd met men like Herman Harcourt throughout my young life. Yes, we Negroes were cursed, but I'd been schooled to break the spell; to confound expectations by exchanging the factory floor (which had been the lot of my parents) for medical school. That was the assumption that had been deeply invested in me. Perhaps it had once been invested in Herman too, but he had defaulted to that older, more persistent preconception of our limitations. If Negroes were cursed, then men such as Herman were carriers of, and became, the virus. If he was the virus, I was the vaccine. The bag man's presence though – his very being – mocked the notion that my contemporaries and I could escape the accursed path predetermined for black people.

Herman's eyes blazed with passionate intensity as he continued, with a note of compunction in his voice, 'They'll be coming for you in the afternoon. If not today, then tomorrow.'

'We are the Ocean, you are the sea,' chanted a group of lads as they joined the number 25 bus at Stepney. The Ocean, the name of their gang, referred to the Ocean Estate, which was made famous by the local R&B singer Leslie Charles, a Trinidadian migrant who tipped his hat to the place he grew up by taking as his performing name: Billy Ocean.

'We are the Ocean, you are the sea, sea, sea,' they continued to chant. They were loud but harmless mostly, though I recognised one or two who were a menace to cyclists. It was always a risk to ride along Mile End Road as the schools got out. Kids from the Ocean would wait at the bus stop to shower any 'middle-class bike-riding wanker' with gobs of spit as they passed by.

Thankfully, they didn't recognise me off the bike. My medical student eyes were in a steady state of readiness, on the lookout for individual forms of pathology. I clocked a schizophrenic as soon as he got on at the next stop. Black and older than average, he shuffled along like a child in his father's slippers. He stepped through the doors in the middle of an intense conversation, although he had no companion. A new idea seemed to come to him with every breath. I had the feeling that he was trying urgently to exhale unpleasant thoughts. He breathed in, he breathed out. He breathed in . . . He started to flounder. His arms flapped. He spun around. 'Please, somebody. Help. I can't . . . I can't breathe.'

No help arrived, and I had no intention of intervening, but

eventually the hyperventilation subsided. It was difficult to read what was going on. The man's face was obscured by sunglasses and a huge floppy cap (the type worn by Rastas), though he seemed to have little hair. Trapped food had dried on the beginnings of a beard.

People moved back into their seats, further than was necessary, drawing their coats more tightly around them as he moved down the aisle. The pall of lost ambition, suggested by his clumsy oversized jacket and stiff, stained trousers in need of a wash, was communicated even more fiercely in the assembly of plastic bags containing the detritus of life – books, rags, clothing and sandwiches that were turning green – that he gripped in each hand. He was followed down the aisle by a small-boned builder, his face cracked and speckled with plaster. The builder stared disapprovingly as the schizophrenic took occupancy of a pair of seats.

'Not too clever, is it, mate?'

It'd been a long day, and he'd had to put up with enough shit already, thank you, and he was minded to exert his native right to a seat in his own fucking country. He pushed aside the schizophrenic's bags. He didn't care if the brown brother stank worse than rancid Gorgonzola or that there were fossilised woodlice in his turn-ups. He was going to take his birthright, what his grandfather fought Hitler for: a seat, mate, all the fucking way to Aldgate.

The schizophrenic moved out of the seat to make room for him. Through the sunglasses his searching eyes caught mine and before I could look away, he had worked his way to the seat beside me. In a sea of miserable faces, my determinedly neutral expression must have seemed comforting, not to mention my colour. It was only then that I recognised him, yet he seemed unaware of who I was.

'Countryman, how far this bus reach?' he asked.

It was hard to believe that this was the same man I'd met the week before; astonishing that he could have deteriorated so much and so fast. Everything about him repelled, but more than that, I was acutely aware of his colour – black like me – and wished he wasn't. For a moment I contemplated speaking French and feigning ignorance of English, but faltered at the end.

'Where are you heading?' I whispered.

'Port of Spain. That's Trinidad,' he added.

'Are you kidding?' I smiled.

'It look like I joke to you? It seem I say it a joke?'

There was no mistaking his seriousness. 'No, no,' I answered. 'You look deadly earnest.'

'But wait!' He pulled up smartly and said, ever so slowly, 'Ernest my middle name.'

'I'm sure it is, Herman.'

'What the rass! How you know my name?'

It was then that I decided that I couldn't stay in the conversation any longer. I stood up, inched past him and pulled the string cord overhead to signal to the driver that I needed to get off at the next stop.

'We are the Ocean, you are the sea!' The gang renewed their chant.

The chanting caught Herman's attention. He looked up from smoothing his plastic bags.

'Noooo,' he smiled. 'It's "That was the river, this is the sea", isn't it?'

The gang stopped their chant. One of the members peeled away and moved down the aisle, pointing towards Herman. 'Cunt!' he said, and the others took the cue for this new chant. 'Cunt! Cunt! Cunt!'

The bus pulled up at the next stop and I disembarked at Stepney Green without giving enough thought to what might happen next. Some of the gang were black, so Herman should have been all right. But for about five minutes I didn't turn around, not for fear that Herman had followed me, but out of worry that he hadn't; that he was still on the bus with the Ocean.

'Before we start,' said the patient. 'Just one t'ing. I not gwan have your finger up me arse.'

The GP looked up from his desk, closing one unwieldy bundle of notes and opening another. 'Ah, good morning, Mr Harcourt.'

'Promise!' said Herman. He was sickly, thin, with a scruffier beard than when we'd last met. I was less sure of how old he might be, as he was one of those men whose body had resisted middle age and was only now beginning to turn. His brown skin was younger than his years; smooth except for a line of suspicion that marked the brow of a hyper-expressive face, fit for a mime artist.

'Say it, say it or write it down,' barked Herman. 'I will not poke me finger up Mr Harcourt arse.'

'Oh, I shouldn't think that'll be necessary,' the doctor assured.

'Why not?'

'Now Herman . . .' Dr Gordon half turned to me. There was the faintest suggestion of a raised eyebrow. He flicked through his notes attempting, but not quite managing, to disguise his boredom. There was a forced quality to the action; more, I felt, for the appearance of thoroughness than the expectation of some sudden insight. 'So Mr Harcourt, what can I do for you today?'

Mr Harcourt's mind was elsewhere. He had only just noticed me, and he looked alarmed.

'This is . . . What was your name again?' asked Dr Gordon.

'Grant,' I said.

'Grant, that's right. This is Grant from the medical school. He'll be sitting in on the surgery for a few days.'

'A junior doctor?'

'Yes, a medical student. A first-year medical student, actually. Rather unusual. Don't ordinarily let them loose on the public so early. We're privileged to have him at the surgery today. Young Grant here must be something special.'

I had become accustomed to the admiration of black people whenever they heard of my beautiful career and I was quite skilled at adjusting my expression to evince the appropriate degree of racial pride and humility. But Herman looked incredulous, even hostile. Nothing in his eyes suggested that he recognised me. He lifted his chin and spoke in a jumble of words that appeared to be from a made-up African language, or an approximation of one. Dr Gordon just about managed to suppress a smile, and encouraged his patient to sit down. After a while, keeping the full beam of his eyes fixed on me, Herman reached out, gripped the rim of the chair and worked his way into the seat.

'Have you check him paper qualification?' Herman asked, cupping his mouth with his hand, before whispering to Dr Gordon, 'You know what them like. Could-a pick it up at Brixton Market.'

I waited for Dr Gordon to intercede, but he merely smiled the way a dog owner might do when their pet jumps up at you. There was also the possibility that he felt it was an argument between two black people and that he was disqualified from intervening. My doubts about Dr Gordon had surfaced that morning, starting with the red Porsche parked outside. This was not Knightsbridge; this was Bromley-by-Bow. He might have been forgiven the signet ring worn on the little finger of his right hand and the manicured fingernails, but the Porsche seemed a vulgar display of wealth in such a poor area.

I should have stood up for myself, but in the midst of arranging the sentences in my head, Herman was given a plastic pot and asked to produce a sample of urine, and instead of retiring to the toilets he simply pulled out his penis and filled the pot. Even after nearly a year at medical school, that fell outside the spectrum of what we had come to expect. And yet again Dr Gordon reacted as if it were no more unexpected than a dog cocking his leg at a tree. I did little to disguise my abhorrence. I like to think it signalled one of those moments of forfeiture when the brother 'tek the shame'. But I couldn't really be sure that anything had passed between us because Herman only had eyes for Dr Gordon. It was apparent that he'd been in and around hospitals over the years. He laid before the doctor a catalogue of ailments in just such a manner as I had seen and heard senior registrars do when summarising a patient's condition to the consultant on a ward round. Using language that was both precise and highfalutin, he spoke with the relish of a man who has been starved of intellectual company.

My scalp began to itch. I had the peculiar sensation that Herman, though speaking to the GP, was actually addressing me; that there were hidden messages that would be undetected by Dr Gordon; that it was a form of code black people adopted when white people were present. I hadn't heard Herman articulate a specific complaint other than that he wasn't feeling right. 'Something is wrong,' was as far as he was able, or prepared, to venture when asked, and yet the GP was already scribbling on a prescription form and ticking boxes on it.

'Working?'

Herman didn't answer.

'When was the last time you worked?'

'When was the last time . . .' Herman broke off and then continued, 'you worked?'

Dr Gordon laughed, thought about it again and laughed some more. He tore the prescription note from the pad in a single unbroken movement that brought to mind someone peeling a plaster from a healed cut. He held out the note for Herman and, for the first time all morning, the doctor smiled with conviction. 'Don't let the buggers grind you down.'

Herman still wouldn't look my way as he prepared to leave and I, equally, couldn't bring myself to look at him. But just before he reached the door, he turned and mumbled some more Africanesque at me; then he was gone.

'Quite the scholar, our Herman,' said Dr Gordon, clicking the top back on his fountain pen after finishing up the notes. I had thought so too, in the way he'd used a battery of words – 'distempered', 'dyspeptic', 'ennui' and 'egress' – that were unfamiliar to me.

'Yes, he certainly has a wide vocabulary,' I agreed.

'No, I mean literally. A linguist, I think. Hence the Kiswahili. He has a PhD.'

'A PhD?' I immediately regretted the incredulity in my voice.

'Unless he bought it at Brixton Market. Ha ha ha! But no, Dr Herman Harcourt used to be a university lecturer. Pitiful really.'

I could hear a stream of Kiswahili now on the other side of the wall, but not consistently so. The Kiswahili morphed into Jamaican patois and then back again. What had puzzled me before about Herman's accent was how it ranged around the Caribbean islands. It wasn't specific. What Dr Gordon said now made sense. There was a performative quality to Herman's speech; a kind of playful ventriloquism. But whether it was Kiswahili, Jamaican or Trinidadian, there was no mistaking the bite of argument and irritation in his haranguing conversation with the receptionist next door. The receptionist wanted him to move on; he was reluctant to leave. When Dr Gordon asked me to find out what was going on, I had a sense that Herman was playing for time and actually waiting for me.

I'd have liked to have gone to him and drawn up a couple of chairs so that we could sit and talk softly. I'd have apologised for abandoning him to his fate on the number 25 the month or so before; I'd have confessed that when I observed him closely I had the queer feeling of looking into a mirror of the projected future, of perhaps seeing how easily his fall could be a rehearsal for my own. I said none of these things.

The traffic was backed up to the east all along the road just past Brick Lane, close to Aldgate East. Motorists leaned out of driver-side windows, craning their necks to try to see what the hell was going on. Three police cars approached the Tube station, surrounding a bus, which appeared to have broken down; more police cars were arriving – with their sirens blaring – inching their way past the stationary traffic. The passengers spilled out from the bus onto the pavement. The driver stepped out too and, bizarrely, seconds later the doors closed behind him and the bus lurched forward.

I struggled to get through the mass of people blocking the entrance to the station. Such was the density that for more minutes than I was comfortable with I couldn't move at all. Without my prompting, one of the passengers said, 'Some loon trying to get to Trinidad or somewhere. I dunno. Daft bugger's gone and hijacked the bus.'

But the hijacking was cut short that instant when half a dozen policemen stormed the bus. Seconds later a couple of officers got off the 25 with a wild-eyed black man who was armlocked between them. An ironic cheer went up from the people on the pavement. I pressed on through the melee, determined not to look back towards the bus, and eventually broke free from the crowd into the atrium of the Tube station. As I descended the steps to the platforms of the station, I heard the hijacker cry out, 'I know that man! I know that man!'

Built originally as a workhouse in the nineteenth century, St Clement's psychiatric hospital had a twelve-foot-high perimeter wall and a heavy wrought-iron gate as a further safeguard against escape. I had been assigned to 'special', that is, to look after just one patient; to act almost as a 'professional friend or chaperone'. The patient had been sectioned months before (the term of his legally binding involuntary incarceration had expired), but he'd since developed anxiety about leaving the grounds of the hospital, even about leaving the ward. I was unsurprised to learn the name of the patient. It had begun to seem as if some irresistible outside force was pulling us together.

Herman Harcourt slept soundly in a high bed, covered from head to toe in a single white sheet, shrouded like a mummy. I sat beside the bed and waited for him to wake. A ward porter, a fellow Caribbean kinsman, looked in on the room and, seeing my black face, sidled up to me and burped through Guinness breath, 'Poor man drug up to him eyeball.'

In our previous encounters, Herman had appeared to be continually on the move. Sleep, even if enforced through medication, must surely have come as a release from that febrile state.

An hour passed and I could not resist the temptation to gently pull back the top of the sheet to confirm that it was indeed Herman. Even as he slept I glimpsed, as I had on that first occasion at Whitechapel almost a year before, the air of a man in exile or retreat from himself, and one who was not yet fully cognisant of the fact. After another hour he began to stir.

'I didn't think you were ever going to wake up,' I said.

Herman yawned, shedding the residue of sleep. 'Man nah dead; coffin nah sell.' His eyes swept round the room. Saliva had been pouring from the edges of his mouth. I reached into a pocket, pulled out a handkerchief and handed it to him.

'You're giving me this?' He began to cry. Tears of appreciation streamed down his cheeks. 'You're really giving this to me?'

The door to the dormitory was ajar, and he asked me to close it. When I returned to his bedside, he was beaming.

'Man, I knew you'd come.'

'You knew?'

'How did you get in?' he whispered. 'What's the plan?'

I told that him that he was confused; that I probably wasn't who he thought I was.

'Of course,' said Herman. 'I get it.' He put his index finger to his lips. 'Shhhhh, we mustn't let on. You're a stranger to me.'

'I am a stranger to you.'

'Yes man, me understand. So what's the plan? You give a sign or signal? I wait for the signal?'

After a while, I managed (and this would be the case in subsequent weeks in Herman's company) to turn the argument. I suggested we go for a walk where he could clear his thoughts; it was to be the first of many, designed progressively to wean him back into society, to overcome his agoraphobia. On day one we walked out of the grounds down Mile End Road for a hundred yards and then returned to St Clements. On day two we doubled the distance, and on day three we trebled it.

At first I was, I confess, embarrassed to walk with him, especially after being instructed by the ward sister to link arms in case he was suddenly overcome by an urge to run off. In many of the shops Herman's reputation for soliciting credit and reneging on payment preceded him. Whenever we approached a grocer's, tobacconist's or off-licence, Herman agitated to switch sides so that he could be closer to the road and buffered by me if he was spotted by one of the irate and unforgiving shopkeepers.

In walking with Herman along Mile End Road it was possible to gauge the stages of his pathology through the landscape. From Grove Road west to Cambridge Heath, I logged the scholarship boy's ruined ambition; the Underground station where his voice gave out when he was desperately trying to busk; the crossroads by the oval synagogue where he caused a massive blockade by standing in the middle of the street to direct the traffic; the Radio Rentals store where he had begged for the first time from a startled young black man who placed a coin in his hand.

My initial reluctance to be associated with Herman stemmed from his lamentable condition. It served as a reminder of my own frailties and the pressure I felt to stick to and stay on the course at medical school, even as evidence came daily that I was unsuited to it; to reward my family's considerable investments (emotional and financial) in me. The yearning to flee from that responsibility was near constant. Herman had clearly escaped his own familial expectations by taking flight into madness.

With time I found myself looking forward to our promenades and peculiar conversations, often punctuated by lucid intervals when Herman cast me as the son he'd never had, a son who might learn from his wisdom and mistakes. And slowly my outlook began to shift from 'thinking pathology' to considering the pathos of Herman's predicament – though he would have rounded on me ('Save your tears for the deserving,' he'd say) if ever I nudged the conversation towards any expression of pity or compassion.

One late afternoon, spying an acquaintance in the distance, whom he was keen to avoid, we took a detour from our normal route and ended up on a back street in Stepney Green where Herman had a council flat. He still had a key and persuaded me to make a pit stop to gather a few possessions. We had to force ourselves in, past piles of unwashed clothes and half-eaten plates of furry and crusted food. I could only speculate about the unhygienic awfulness of the toilet because Herman was adamant that it was out of order. Then, having gathered a bundle of shirts and trousers from the flat, and despite my protestations that we were already late for returning to St Clements, Herman refused to leave. When I asked him when he would be ready, he answered, 'Never.'

Here was the moment I had always feared when accompanying Herman – a shearing away from our shared reality and a turn towards an interim state that might lead to a florid psychosis. That 'never' seemed to come from somewhere and someone else. Almost in the same breath, Herman beckoned me over to the bed to help him lift the mattress. Underneath were a slew of dirty magazines. That was to be expected, but in between the copies of Men Only and Penthouse were clumps of £10 and £20 notes. As I lifted the mattress, Herman swept them all into a plastic bag. There must have been more than £1,000.

I should have jumped in and said something, anything. In

my stupefaction, Herman laid out the most ridiculous plan, fuelled by a mania that suggested his mood-regulating medication was wearing off. He could not return to the hospital. To go back was to confine himself to loss, to no life; he would never be considered sane again. The only sensible course of action would be to take the money and fly back to Antigua, from where he had arrived thirty-five years before. It made perfect sense, didn't it? And I could go back with him. In any event, we could discuss the details en route, on the bus, the Underground and the plane. We had to get to Heathrow fast before his/our absence was detected – because we were in this together now and there was no going back. None whatsoever.

Herman was out the front door before I could process any of what he was saying. I followed lamely in a daze as he made his way to the Underground, first onto the District Line and then changing to the Circle. We spoke non-stop; but I was aware that I argued unconvincingly, because some part of me was attracted to the folly, to the roll of the dice, to jacking it all in and not answering to anyone. Round and round we went on the Circle Line, perhaps three times before the realisation, like a cold snap in the pit of the stomach, began to sink in that all this talk was madness.

'Is this it?' Herman asked every few stops. I shook my head and brushed away the tears that had started to come. Somehow, after yet another circumnavigation of the Circle Line and then back onto the District Line, I managed to convince Herman that we'd arrived at the stop for Heathrow and not in fact, at Mile End. 'Quick time, quick time,' I encouraged Herman as we hurried off the carriage and out of the Underground. It was only when we emerged onto the street that Herman understood my treachery. 'Negroes are cursed!' he screamed. 'Negroes are cursed!' He fled before I could lock arms with him. He moved with surprising speed, shuffling along quickly with short steps. Just a few hundred yards away, though, he pulled up abruptly. He seemed unconvinced. Having made too good a job of his escape, he now looked worried that he'd not be caught.

Above the roar of traffic, Herman hesitated. He'd have been swept up into the air by the wind if there was any; he could go neither forwards nor backwards. He froze in front of a street lamp. It was dusk, and the lamplight began to fail, to give out – on, off, on, off . . . He tried to work out the sequence of the code. He counted the beats between each glink. But no matter how hard Herman willed the sequence to continue, the lapse between each surge of light grew longer until the street lamp finally, stubbornly, refused to restart, its message left incomplete.

I caught up with him and led him towards the hospital. He recoiled, pulling against me, groaning, 'Merciful Lord, help!', but really, he put up limited resistance and quickly gave in to the inevitable, surrendered as he knew he must, as he so often had, to the greater will, to the allure of someone with a clearer sense of the way ahead.

Ethlyn

Wheel and come again

Sometimes I wondered: what if I had succumbed to Herman's wish and gone with him to the Caribbean? What then? I suppose I'd at least have been forced to make the decision that I took five years later, to leave medicine entirely. Soon after that final encounter with Herman Harcourt, I boarded a plane to the Caribbean on my own, to visit Jamaica for the first time. I told myself that I'd gone ahead without Herman, but that one day he'd be recalled and make his own way back. That seductive narrative of return was one that pulled at the heart of most of the West Indians I'd grown up with. Ethlyn was forever telling us, 'Don't get too comfortable, you know, 'cause one day we're going back, yes man!' But it never happened; she never left Luton. By 1994, though, I'd made up my mind that the dream would no longer be deferred.

Somehow Pauline Adams and her tribe, the Adams family, learned that I planned to take Ethlyn back to Jamaica. That's when the phone calls began. My aunt Monique, whom I hadn't spoken to for almost a decade, rang to remind me that Ethlyn, her eldest sister, hadn't returned home to the Caribbean island since she left thirty-five years ago. Was I aware that it was bound to prove stressful for her? Monique has an unfortunate, nasal voice, so even when she wasn't attempting to be haughty, you were immediately put on your mettle. She spoke in a non-stop monologue, weaving a fine tapestry of nothing: words that were essentially the same point about trauma over and over again. 'Are you still there?' she said finally, when I didn't immediately respond. 'Colin, are you there?'

Apart from Uncle Castus, I had never been conscious of my aunts' and uncles' interest in their sister's welfare. Rather, spearheaded by Pauline Adams, they'd mostly only ever expressed their indifference towards Ethlyn. 'How did you get this number?' I asked.

Monique sighed. 'I don't have time for this.'

'You rang me!'

'You're a bright boy. Have a think about what I've said. Have a think.' Monique put the phone down before I could.

That wouldn't be the last of it, I realised. Once they perceived you as the enemy or even a future threat, like their TV counterparts, the only way you could disabuse a member of the Adams family of that notion would be to drive a stake through their heart, bolt down their coffin and lower them into a grave later filled with lead. Monique, unsurprisingly, rang again the next day.

'You have a duty of care,' My aunt was pained to point out. 'Your mother? She's an elderly woman. You're being irresponsible, forcing her to go back, taking her all that way. Say something happened . . . ?' This time, I replaced the receiver first.

'Who are you planning on seeing when you're out there?' Monique squawked down the phone another day later.

'What's it to you?'

'What's it to me?' Her voice edged towards irritation. 'Why can't you answer a simple question?'

'Because it's not a simple question.'

I avoided picking up the next couple of days and was sad to have forgotten my pledge to myself when the phone sounded on Friday.

'You do realise they're holding up and killing returnees in Jamaica?' I imagined Monique smiling into the mouthpiece. 'You can go to Jamaica, but you might not come back. Well, if you do come back, it'll be in a wooden box.'

A few days later I was in the air, on a plane bound for Jamaica. Ethlyn sat beside me, with my wife, Jo, our two-year-old daughter, Jazz and my brother, Chris seated on the other side of the aisle.

To 'wheel and come again' is to turn around. Imagine you're on the road, driving. It occurs to your passenger that she's forgotten something. Brother, you may think you've gone too far to head back, but she commands, 'wheel and come again, man!' It's not up for discussion. You thread the steering wheel through your hands; you execute a U-turn, nice and easy on the smooth asphalt road, and head back to where you came from. Throughout my childhood, I could never hear that phrase without pondering Ethlyn's unrealised desire to 'wheel and come again' in her life, to return to Jamaica, the place of her birth. It wasn't just that the expense was prohibitive. I suspect she feared something that could not be named: an encounter with her former self along the way.

Our house and life in the 1970s was marked by much upheaval. But there was one constant: *The Gleaner*. Every Friday, Jamaica's national newspaper made its way over 4,000 miles from the capital, Kingston, to 42 Castle Croft Road, Luton. It gave me a headache as a child, when I stopped and thought about it. The journey always seemed dizzyingly impossible, something of a miracle, when I imagined the steps from the printing press in Jamaica: the newspaper bundle flung into the back of a van, stacked in the hold of a plane, and then unloaded onto another van in England, before wending its way on the road to Luton. Brother Williams was the final link in the chain. It was always a delight to open the front door to the Jamaican elder. Brother Williams had a smile like he'd seen heaven, and I came to associate Jamaica with that smile. He delivered *The Gleaner* to our house each time as if its safe passage was his personal responsibility. There was something furtive in the way he'd appear like clockwork on a Friday afternoon to hand-deliver the paper, as if he feared it falling into the wrong hands. Perhaps it was just a personality trait. For apart from being the nicest man in the world, Brother Williams was also the most reliable.

I never saw Bageye ever read, or even pick up *The Gleaner*. Why would he? There was no news about race meetings or whether that 'damn crook' Lester Piggott, the jockey who he lost the most money on, was riding. It was Ethlyn who subscribed to *The Gleaner*. Our mother had long ago given up on the expensive pleasure of Silk Cut or Embassy Number 1 cigarettes, and her Wednesday Bingo nights with her Irish girlfriends were only now and then, but she would never forgo the precious weekly missive from Jamaica.

Ethlyn left Jamaica for England in 1959. The passport photo from that time is misleading. She was twenty-six when she arrived; the photo was taken earlier when Ethlyn, aged nineteen, was due to depart for a new life in New York, after an aunt in Harlem agreed to sponsor her. But something went wrong; the trip was vengefully cancelled, in the fallout from a family feud, it seems. Ethlyn rarely spoke about it. The venture to the UK seven years later was something of a consolation prize. And yet there's a look of defiance and resignation in her young eyes – as if she foresaw in 1952 that Luton, rather than Harlem, would be her eventual destination.

Soon after she arrived, Ethlyn's grip was shoved on top of the wardrobe, and there it remained. It was still in place thirty-five years later. The grip had a menacing and accusing presence. It was the one item in the house that we were forbidden from even touching. It was tempting, of course, but the best way to resist temptation is to give in to it. Surely, I'd often berate myself in front of the bathroom mirror, you'd no more take down the grip and force it open than you'd break a lock on someone's personal diary to read it. Only a morally bankrupt villain would do such a thing. At Saturday morning confession, Father Quinn's silence was more damning than the sentence of extra Hail Marys.

Each time, maybe once a year, I pried open the lock with a pair of scissors when I couldn't locate the hidden key. I was convinced I'd find a secret, that opening up the lid would release Ethlyn's true thoughts. Yes, I imagined her whispers and sighs escaping the grip. But I could never really make sense of the bric-a-brac, receipts, thin airmail letters from Jamaica and postcards that filled the case and never seemed to change from one break-in till the next.

The grip lay between my mother and me, no matter our intimacy; it was a mark of her distance and unfathomableness. Like so many of her contemporaries, she'd packed her bags with a promise to always return to Jamaica. The catch may have been faulty, but the grip was there, ready on top of the wardrobe, just waiting for the word. The word never came, but the call did, from the pages of *The Gleaner*, like a siren song that Ethlyn tried to block out, but could not resist.

After running through a long list of instructions and getting us to repeat them back to her word perfectly, – 'Don't answer the door; Chris must put on his scarf; make sure the immersion switch is off!' – Ethlyn would leave through the front door for work at Vauxhall Motors. She'd always return through the back door. I guess it had something to do with superstition. At about 4 p.m. on Friday afternoon, our mother would barely have taken off her coat before she sat down at the dining table and spread out *The Gleaner*. She'd make a respectful show of taking an interest in the current affairs articles. Often from the back of her throat there'd be the sad disbelieving sound, unique to her 'hmm mmh' about one of the news items. I'd ask her: 'What? What is it?'

'Just some man chop up him wife,' came the reply. 'Them people carry on bad.' To my look of horror, she'd offer limited reassurance: 'Bad-minded people? You have them anywhere you go.'

And with some relief, then, she'd turn to the back page, calling for a pencil, and then a sharpener.

The back page of *The Gleaner* was always covered with adverts from estate agents selling homes in Jamaica or sometimes with architectural drawings of the modern-looking houses to be built on plots of land for sale. Attractions included living rooms that offered: carpeted comfort; helpers' rooms; an acre or more of land which ominously was also 'entirely grilled', and a nearby white sandy beach, strangely called 'Hellshire', though Ethlyn said the paper had it wrong: everyone knew it as 'Healthshire'.

I willed my mum to make a pencil-mark beside the property that was close to the beach, but she hesitated. 'Can't see me there,' she snorted, not kind of, but actually snorted. 'I would never live it down. They're not my kind of people. You have to know your people. I can't be a hypocrite.'

Ethlyn preferred a place called Mandeville. She'd never been, she said, 'But I hear it cool up there, nice and cool. You have to take a jumper.' She held the pencil, hesitating about where she should place the cross, beside which advert for a home or piece of land. Her deliberation reminded me of Bageye's seriousness as he daily pored over the horses in the *Sporting Life*, calculating which horse and jockey to back, and whether to bet 'to win' or 'each way'. Ethlyn's choice, though, was not merely a gamble on a horse, but a possible investment in our future. It weighed heavily on her as she called for a rubber to erase the X and find a better prospect.

Each Friday she'd begin again; but no down payment was ever made. It took me years to realise that the business with *The Gleaner* was just window-shopping; it was a fantasy. She never seemed frustrated though, and neither, finally, were we because any discontent was drowned out each Friday afternoon by her hum of happiness.

The years stretched to over a decade, but then, sometime in the 1980s, *The Gleaner* stopped arriving. I feared Brother Williams had died, but later I heard that he'd gone back to Jamaica – for good. Someone else could have delivered *The Gleaner* of course, but when I asked about it, Ethlyn answered that she didn't 'business with that again'.

Ethlyn would take down the grip occasionally and examine the contents. It was always an intensely private moment, like prayer. I tried not to pass the room, as she sat with the case open in front of her. But if ever I did, and caught her eye, she'd smile and whisper: 'Bwoi, poverty is a terrible thing.' It was a statement of fact – she had come down in the world from the middle-class comforts she'd imagined her future to be when in Jamaica – but also as a refrain, part of a warning. 'I was too proud. Look at me now.'

Then I proposed a plan for her to go back, if only for a visit to Jamaica. Three decades after my mother left the island, I'd accompany her on the return leg and make a BBC radio documentary about it. Remarkably, she said yes. Perhaps I should not have been surprised. 'I have my suitcase ready from time,' she said. 'Look from when!'

After Monique's phone call of death foretold, we didn't hear from her again. I went back to Luton to help Ethlyn prepare. News of her imminent return to Jamaica soon spread round the West Indian circles in Luton; she was inundated with requests to 'tek back a likkle somethin' for various uncles, aunts, parents. On her last Sunday, a day or two before departure, Pastor Blake invited Ethlyn onto the platform at Dale Road Pentecostal Church (by then we'd left Catholicism behind), and presented her to the congregation as if she was a prisoner, a lifer who had miraculously been granted parole. Someone broke into the hymn 'This World is Not My Resting Place' and whoops of joy and 'Hallelujahs' reverberated round the hall. Pastor Blake called for a love offering, and the church brothers and sisters dug deep into their pockets and purses to fill the collection plate.

A week before departure for the airport, there were still a handful of matters to attend to. Chief among them was my mother's unexpected concerns about her hair. It was surprising because Ethlyn had what she considered 'good hair', loose, not natty 'bad hair'. The good hair, though, was thinning a little on top, and, hearing about her discomfort, Selma, who was still aloof but would phone occasionally, had by then landed a good job as an 'art buyer' (whatever that meant) at Saatchi & Saatchi, and offered to buy her a hair piece which could be sewn in.

My eldest sister's once-in-a-decade heroics usually came with a catch, exposing the gulf between her overly ambitious intent and the reality. Selma's Hollywood blockbuster budget for a real hairpiece was quickly scaled back to funds allowing for a more affordable synthetic one. Too late did Ethlyn learn that synthetic hair was only washable if you didn't mind the explosive and unwieldy mess that would result from its introduction to water. A pair of scissors was needed to excise the offending mess, and now there was no option but to wear a wig.

Her tears might have been of frustration, but I hadn't expected the emotional transformation in a woman whose approach to hair and make-up was usually never more than perfunctory. In the past, when pushed to explain why, Ethlyn would answer that obviously, she was attractive: 'tree nah grow in my face'.

She never failed to make an effort, though it wasn't always appreciated. I still recall, like an acidic reflux, St Columba's College's 1979 Dinner and Dance, the highlight of the social calendar for the well-heeled, middle-class parents of boys at the school. I was head boy that year, and tradition required that the former head boy's father, Mr Jenkins, would lead the dancing by inviting the present head boy's mother, Ethlyn, for the first waltz.

By 1979, my mother had shown Bageye the door. That night, though intimidated by the invitation to be a guest of honour at the high table, Ethlyn had been game enough to attend the Dinner and Dance. This, after all, was at some level what she had dreamed and worked for, grabbing all the overtime at the factory she could get: a son making his way in high society; you couldn't get higher than the high table.

Ethlyn, in her Sunday best, was escorted by her Irish friend from work, Anne Hegarty. I can still picture the self-conscious way that both women fidgeted with their cloth napkins as they ate and the sound of the heavy knives and forks, scraping the expensive-looking plates.

There was an expanding 'hushhhhh' across the hall when the music changed, announcing the waltz, but Mr Jenkins, comfortable in his dinner jacket, hesitated. He glanced briefly at the working-class black woman across from him, whom he was to partner; his face was flushed with uncertainty. Mr Jenkins, who up till then had been the picture of politeness, did not stand and hold out his hand. But before the waltz ended, as I remember, Anne Hegarty stood and holding out her hand said, 'C'mon Lynn,' and proceeded to the dance floor for a waltz with my mum. It sounds like a triumph, but when I revisit the memory now, I can't locate that emotion.

Putting on the wig the right way round or back-to-front seemed to make little difference. No matter how many times she adjusted it, the damn wig mocked her; it could not be tamed. I struggled to mask my alarm as she prepared for the final Sunday church service.

Ethlyn would never have countenanced wearing false hair amongst the church sisters of Dale Road, but something in her was shifting as we approached the date we were due to fly, an unspoken anxiety whose roots – because she testily brushed aside my questions – I didn't understand. And when I passed her bedroom that night to see her kneeling – elbows on the bed, in prayer – for the first time, I wavered in my commitment to what Monique had called the unnecessary trauma of Ethlyn's return to Jamaica. I knocked on the bedroom door, 'Everything all right?'

'I wonder if we should call it off?' she said. 'My bad eye a-dance.'

Jamaica is 'no place like home' proclaimed the 1960s Tourist Board film Ethlyn and I watched on a VHS cassette the night before our trip. 'No place like home' because it was unusual, an idyllic, tropical paradise, a relief from the grey, forbidding, low-hanging clouds of Britain. Ethlyn nodded all the way through the film. There really was no place better than home, and finally, after three decades, she'd be able to appreciate that simple truth. It wasn't so simple. When I was twenty, I'd visited the island by myself and, though thrilled and energised by the vivaciousness of the people and the gorgeous, fecund landscape, I often struggled to make sense of Jamaica's peculiarity. Strangers in the street seemed 'extra' or unnecessarily performative. I was unnerved not just by the everyday flamboyant theatricality but by the spectacular poverty of the many docile, semi-naked vagrants who didn't even bother to beg. I was ashamed about my timidity when walking downtown in the capital; for I could never really rid myself of the feeling of dread and menace. I said none of this to Ethlyn.

She was excited and anxious all the way through the flight. My mum hadn't been on a plane since leaving Jamaica for Britain in 1959. She was touched, surprised even, by the simple courtesies of the air stewards. In contrast to her usual interactions with English people, the stewards, swishing down the aisles in effortless glamour, seemed genuine in their concern to accommodate her every need. Ethlyn tested them regularly as they passed, and they answered immediately, fetching whatever she demanded. 'They have manners,' said Ethlyn approvingly.

Good manners on British Airways, but rudeness on Air Jamaica when we transferred at Miami for the final leg of the journey. The stewards' surliness might have been explained by the headline in *The Gleaner*, 'Air J cutting loose ageing flight attendants'. Once a Jamaican air steward reached thirty, she was gone. The news suggested, worryingly, that it was not a country for old people; in particular for a woman, now in her early sixties, who, I would soon discover, harboured thoughts of starting all over again.

Ethlyn adjusted her face, like an actor getting into character, as we stepped off the plane, and inched through customs, eventually to be catapulted into baggage claim. Only one conveyor belt seemed to be in operation in the high-ceilinged hall. It mostly clattered along empty because each time luggage appeared a porter reached over to pull it off the belt and heft it onto a growing mountain of suitcases. 'Hmm mmh. You see how dem stay?' said Ethlyn, eyeing the teetering edifice. 'Not a t'ing change.'

As well as the familiar shock of heat outside the terminal, there was a wall of people to greet new arrivals. Jamaica is the loudest place on earth, and all the voices, radios and sound systems were turned up beyond eleven. Ethlyn didn't seem too disturbed by the ruck of taxi drivers vying for our custom. A young boy emerged from the scrum and tried to extract one of Ethlyn's bags from her hand. She gripped all the more tightly. 'Sorry mother,' he said. 'You want taxi? My uncle have taxi.'

'Him have seat belt?' asked Ethlyn.

The boy nodded.

'Then mek him come.'

The taxi-driving uncle must have been observing the exchange because he was at our side before the boy had taken two steps in his direction. The uncle surprised me by answering 'Mr Campbell' when I asked him his name. He started picking up all our luggage; it didn't seem humanly possible but he managed, refusing my offer to help with even the smallest item.

It was clear after twenty minutes of driving that was like Bageye's walking, just faster than slow, that even though Mr

Campbell had nodded knowingly when we gave him the name and address of our hotel, he really had no clue as to its whereabouts. In hushed tones, Mr Campbell sought direction from an intermediary on the phone. 'Is lost you lost?' asked Ethlyn. Mr Campbell thought it wise not to answer, but a little while later Ethlyn exclaimed, 'You pass it! You jus' pass it.'

Listening to the ease with which Ethlyn talked was remarkable. I'd observed growing up with her in Luton over the years, how she became so fed up with English people saying 'pardon?' to her whenever she opened her mouth that after a while, she stopped speaking with them altogether. Conscious of her accent, whenever the phone rang and some official was on the line, Ethlyn no longer answered but just handed the receiver to me – her child interpreter/translator. Now she spoke freely, as if restored to her mother tongue.

In the years leading up to leaving the island in 1959, Ethlyn's life had been tumultuous. One day her merchant seamen brothers brought home a friend, a steward on their ship. Over dinner, this charming and smartly dressed raconteur even made his unfortunate nickname sound like a badge of honour. For most of the year, Bageye was at sea; when on shore-leave, he tended to stay at seamen's lodges. Now he took to coming round to the Adams house as often as possible, stepping out with Ethlyn. Within a year of their courtship, she became pregnant.

Bageye was once more at sea, physically and metaphorically, when Ethlyn gave birth to Selma at a maternity hospital that locals called the 'Lying-in'. 'I took the baby home with me. What else was I going to do?' Ethlyn told me. On the way to our first destination, Jacques Road, she recounted that becoming an unmarried mother, associated with a man who was just one rung up from a merchant ship's galley boy, had not been the life she'd imagined for herself. 'I was really glamorous back then. I was really attractive, with my long hair, my big earrings and flowers on the side of my hair, my peasant blouse. Oh, I was really something to look at.'

In the late 1940s, the oldest girl of ten siblings, Ethlyn had lived in comfortable middle-class surroundings with her parents. The family's fortunes seemed to have peaked with her father, Vivian Wellington Adams's promotion to Inspector of Police, and their subsequent relocation to Jacques Road in a sought-after residential area.

Once the bags were securely checked in at our hotel and I'd hired a more suitable mode of transport, we decided that the family house in Jacques Road would be our first stop. Chris sat upfront in the passenger seat. Jo volunteered to drive so that I could sit in the back and record my mum's reflections in real time. Jazz was buckled into in her child seat between us. I noticed that even though we were not due to meet any relatives yet, Ethlyn had put on one of her best outfits. She craned her neck as the car sped along, trying to take in all the sights and sounds.

'This can't be it,' said my mum, as Jo pulled up on Jacques Road and turned off the engine. 'Go on a little bit, just to be sure.'

'No Mum,' I said, 'This is it.'

'Jacques Road?'

'Yes.'

Ethlyn was robust and healthy, but some paralysis temporarily gripped her. Jo jumped out and opened the door for her, helping her to slowly emerge from the car. Back in the 1950s, the area had been prosperous; their family had had a maid and a cook. Ethlyn's father had been chauffeured to work, and she'd been so conscious of her standing in society that once, when spotting the family maid downtown on family business, but not wearing her uniform, she'd had the maid fired.

Jacques Road didn't appear to be so prosperous; it wasn't even shabby-chic; the houses looked tired and neglected, and that included Number 2, where Ethlyn and her mother, father and siblings had revelled in the signifying of their upper-middle-class pretensions.

'The foundation is still there, apart from the top,' Ethlyn mused, trying to stem her shock. 'The roof was tiled, now it's zinc, corrugated zinc they call it, but,' she added brightly, 'the structure of the house is still there.'

'It's quite overgrown isn't it. Was it like this in your day?'

'No, no. It wasn't like this at all. Not all these plants, rough plants you know. Ahhh to know that this part of the country is deteriorating like this, is terrible. The street never used to be like this, no man. It was more suburban. It's nearly a ghetto, now. It's actually a ghetto.'

I suggested we take a closer look, even though I was wary of the sign on the fence, which said 'Knock' and 'Beware of bad dogs'.

'It's chained up, but I don't know why,' said Ethlyn. 'We can knock and see if anybody is in.'

Four or five bad dogs rushed yelping to the gates. They were neither big nor scary, and probably not very bad. They were followed by a tiny woman. She had the frame of a child, though her face was heavily lined, her skin like crumpled paper; a housekeeper, I imagined. Even before we announced ourselves and our intention, she flapped her hands, as if trying to free something from the ends of her fingers, attempting to wave us off.

'The owner is away. Mrs Johnson is away,' she said.

I asked Ethlyn if the name meant anything to her.

'No, no no,' she answered distractedly, saying no to more than my question.

'You come for a plant? We don't open yet.'

The woman had been trading in plants for 'quite a while now, but we don't sell very much,' she said. I asked her how long she'd been in the house and I was astonished when she said, 'Going thirty-two years now.' She'd arrived there just a couple of years after Ethlyn had left Jacques Road. I gestured for my mum to come closer and share her story, but she seemed unable or unwilling to talk any further with the old woman. Every time something else caught Ethlyn's eye, all I heard was the familiar 'hmm mmh'.

The housekeeper and I stood on either side of the padlocked gate, like priest and penitent, though I wasn't sure which was my role.

'My mother's saying that she has noticed quite a change in the streets since she lived here.' I pushed even closer forward with my lips touching the fence because the woman seemed to have trouble understanding my accent. 'Has it changed much? The area, has it changed since you've been here?'

'Yes, everything change up, change up, change up, everything. Because all the houses that were along here, they demolish them, so, everything change up. Everything change up. The people dem remove out and the robber dem tear dem down.'

I asked this local historian about the desertion: what had happened to the people who used to live in this area?

'Some gone away to foreign, some to America, some England, Canada, all around.' She was certain: 'They remove and gone out, and when they come back, they don't come back this area again. Dem gone further up the hills, to Upper Meadowbrook and all those places.' Someone called her from within the house and she moved towards it, still talking but her voice fading, fading with her litany of middle-class flight from the area.

At least one of them, though, had 'gone to foreign' and come back. But if Ethlyn was ever to consider making her stay more permanent, it would not be in a house in the 'ghetto' marked by Jacques Road.

'Where next?' I asked, back at the car.

Ethlyn suggested heading to another of her old homes. This time to Outlook Avenue, off the Windward Road. We'd already begun to settle into a nice rhythm with Jo doing all the driving. Jo, whose grace and steadfastness always impressed my mother, was unruffled by the task, made more precarious by the dangerous, idiosyncratic drivers of whom it was said, 'dem drive straight to heaven.' But the sight of our white chauffeur must have proved incongruous to others. Vehicles slowed as we passed, getting a good look in. At traffic lights the gawpers dallied and had to be beeped to move along.

'You see the sea down the end there?' said Mum, with a satisfying hum as we approached Outlook Avenue. 'We live at number eleven, it was. One house was in the back you know, a smaller little house, but we were at the front. A very lovely home. I was around twenty-four, twenty-five when we sold the house in Jacques Road and came down here.'

'But why? It's not very far away,' I said. 'Why did you move?'

Ethlyn looked startled. Couldn't I see? 'This is a better area, even then, than Jacques Road. To be honest, this was a residential area.' She rolled the 'r' in residential dramatically. 'You can see that this is *the* area at that time.'

I was confused, but I didn't let on. I'd been disingenuous with my questions. Other relatives, one or two of Ethlyn's siblings, had told me the exact opposite of Ethlyn's assertion, that the move to Outlook Avenue was not an upgrade: it was most decidedly a downgrade from Jacques Road.

Number two Jacques Road had been the pinnacle of their middle-class respectability. But the decade that followed was one of steady decline, fuelled in part by old man Adams's expensive infidelity; keeping a second home and mistress in luxury meant selling the house at Jacques Road. His wife, Pauline, and children were forced to move several times into increasingly shabbier accommodation. Inspector Adams's neglect was twofold: it consigned his children to poverty, and through the psychological torture of Pauline, it acted as a kind of matrimonial, constructive dismissal.

Jamaicans will tell you that there are no facts, only versions. Whilst I would dispute the notion of no facts, the idea of only versions resonates. I'd always known that our Adams family historians, as was true of all historians really, did not write history; they curated history. And I could see now, on this first day in Kingston, how Aunt Monique's sourness reflected her nervousness that my visit to Jamaica with Ethlyn would mess with her brand of the family's history.

Even if I fully believed the version of the move to Outlook Avenue told to me by Monique, it would have been wrong, cruel actually, to rob Ethlyn of her story. I kept quiet and made appreciative sounds, nodding as my mum spoke.

'Yes, at the end of here we have the sea. That's why these houses are more expensive on account of having the sea down there, the beach down there.'

As we walked to the end of Outlook Avenue towards Bournemouth Beach, we could just make out the remnants of the lido. Back in Ethlyn's time, Bournemouth Beach also gave its name to a grand night club located there, built in the shape of a giant 'S', the dance floor on one level, a double swimming pool on the next, and steps lit by candles leading down to the sea. It would have mirrored the gentility of early Colonial life.

'We always had nice dresses, nice cotton dresses or satin.' Ethlyn appeared to swoon as she spoke. 'It doesn't matter 'cause the evenings are cool and we always wear halter-neck dresses with the back exposed . . . give us the cool breeze. We never wear heavy velvet and things like that. Just nice organdie and voile. Cool materials, nice dresses, and we had Russian sandals that you tie right up to your ankles. And of course the fashionable hairdo and your big jewellry. I love jewels. West Indians on the whole love to have big earrings and bracelets.'

Walking back up Outlook Avenue, another memory came to my mother, its clarity sharpened all the more because it was unbidden.

'I don't remember the exact one of the houses, but I know there was a few, kind of a . . . well, where women . . . these businessmen used to take their girlfriends dinner time; professional men with their secretaries. No riff-raff and no street women, vulgar-looking – always nice groomed girls, secretaries. Under the cover, like. Nobody knew, but the residents knew.'

'Are you saying that was a brothel?'

'Privately owned like you know, not official. You would see all the cars coming dinner time with their secretaries; you know something is going on, but you can't prove it.'

Ethlyn answered my look of scepticism: 'It would happen everywhere you go, you know. These private landlords do their t'ing.'

I listened to my mother but kept quiet. I didn't confess to Ethlyn that Uncle Castus had told me a similar story. But he told me the 'brothel' had been right next door to their house. Nineteen-fifties Jamaica, like Victorian Britain, was not arranged for the benefit of women. When times were rough, many young women – even out-of-work 'nicely groomed secretaries' – might find themselves in the unfortunate position of becoming prostitutes in all but name. High-minded, churchgoing Ethlyn wasn't about to criticise them.

By 1959, Ethlyn, now with a two-year-old child in tow, was on the move again, and still dependent on her family. Earlier in the year, her mother, Pauline, had filed for divorce. When her absent husband heard about it and came to the house armed with a knife, threatening to kill her if she proceeded with the court hearing, she fled with her remaining children to a 'mixed' area called Vineyard Town. They lived in two squalid, cockroach-infested attic rooms, in fear not only of their discovery by the irate Inspector of Police but also of the area's random street violence spilling over into the boarding house whose back door could never be locked properly. Within a few weeks Pauline managed to arrange for their passage to Britain.

Vineyard Town had been a step down from Outlook Avenue. The year Ethlyn left Jamaica, locals had been shocked by reports of a knife attack on a night patrolman guarding a theatre.

Then it was knives, now it was guns. Thirty-five years later, we were greeted by headlines in *The Gleaner* of the recent gruesome discovery in Vineyard Town of a 45-year-old woman and her daughter, whose bodies were found with gunshot wounds to their chests, lying in their living room.

Ethlyn pulled her head back from the page: 'Hmm mmh.' Eventually, she worked her way to the adverts at the back of the paper – still a feature, as they had been when she was a regular subscriber in the 70s.

'Anything take your fancy?' I asked. 'Do you want a pen, to mark it up?'

'No harm in that. Why not? Nothing to keep me in England. What is there in England? You all gone now.'

'I was joking.'

'You don't take life seriously, Colin.'

'Are you serious?'

'You have that pen? Plenty nice houses here. You can come and visit.'

'So long as it's not Vineyard Town.'

On Saturday mornings in Luton, she cleaned the house with a brush and pan, somehow shutting out the disgrace of her impoverished life, reciting Kipling verbatim and crying over the nobility of Gunga Din, whose true value, like hers, went unappreciated by the English.

Back on the road in Jamaica, passing through Vineyard Town, my mum's eyes sought the original buildings, the roads, hills and gullies that she'd known as a child and young adult in Jamaica. She averted her gaze, subtly, from more contemporary structures. She didn't care for the new shopping malls in New Kingston, and she wanted instead to go downtown, just south of Jones Town, to the old commercial centre, now raffish and 'dangerous', if you listened to affluent islanders who never ventured there; a shadow of its former glorious self. Ethlyn's nostalgia was rich; it gave off heat and warmth to those who were close to her. That nostalgic impulse should have made her vulnerable to the violence of change; it did not. As the first week folded into the next, the blip of sorrow manifested at Jacques Road was not repeated. I was astonished by the contrast to the mournfully romantic woman I'd grown up with in England.

Despite the warnings, we headed downtown; my nervousness, I convinced myself, was more a case of worrying for her, Jo, Jazz and Chris than for myself. In truth, I hadn't been able to fully shrug off Monique's warning that we'd return home in coffins. 'I know my people,' Ethlyn laughed at my timidity. 'Them not going to do us no harm.'

Kingston brimmed with vocal and excited crowds. Incidents, you felt, could pop off at any minute. Turning a corner, we saw a screaming man flash by, pursued by another brandishing a cutlass. I looked to Ethlyn with my palms up but she just shrugged. 'Some people always carry on bad,' she said.

'All Port of Spain,' Derek Walcott once mused, 'is a noon-day show.' He was referring to Trinidad's capital, but the sentiment equally applied to Kingston, Jamaica. There was a performative quality to the place.

Down by the harbour, the last hurricane had damaged much of the area, but the remnants of an old craft market were still there, and at least one old sailor waiting for his ship that would never come in.

'The "Grace Lines" from New York City used to come right down here at the craft market and the tourists come off those ships and enjoy themselves, right.' The old seaman was bone-thin, and hadn't seen a dentist in quite a while now. Perhaps seventy, he was an energetic, high-voltage hustler, hard-wired to seek out and exploit every opportunity, but more amusing than pitiably abhorrent. The man was the kind of 'wharf rat' Ethlyn would have shunned in her youth and scolded for the impertinence of thinking he might engage her in conversation. But she seemed immediately fond of him and grateful to him for helping her conjure the past. Four of Ethlyn's brothers had been merchant seamen.

'Yeah, that's right,' she said. 'You would find the sailors on the road walking around when they get their leave, that's right.'

'We had privilege that time.'

'That's right!'

'You could walk in the street at one o'clock at night and nobody interrupt you. Go to dances and everything like that and you are all right, but now, at eight o'clock you have to go home. Gun men. Youth now will cut your throat and take what you got. I witness this my own self because they try it with me also. No soldiers, no police at nights. So, it's just the ragga muffin.'

The old-timer offered to be our guide; he assured me that he wouldn't take up much room in the car, but I said no, wary of the unspoken expectations down the line, even though he was affronted by the suggestion of a price on his sudden friendship.

Jamaica is a tourist island but not many tourists stop at Kingston and fewer still venture into Jones Town, one of the poorest districts in the capital. The streets were a maze of rusting corrugated iron, half-made houses with exposed breeze blocks, dirt roads, all traversed by minibuses, drinks carts, maaga dogs and goats. A succession of young men proposed themselves as our guides; I regretted immediately having turned down the old sailor. Their offer seemed more like a threat, but Ethlyn, stepping in front of me, scattered them with a few loud words. When I professed my amazement at what she'd done, Ethlyn just kissed her teeth.

'I was born here in Jones Town, don't forget. It was here my great-grandmother used to live. Granny Reid we used to call her then. She was a granddaughter of a slave. Gong was a slave and Mamma, then Granny Reid, Isabella Reid. Just three generations down.' This mantra of my mum was familiar to me, but I'd always been frustrated that we never learned more beyond the list of names. We wandered into an open compound. Ethlyn squinted into the past. 'It was much newer than this. It was sixty years ago. Granny Reid had rooms in the back here that she rent out to people and she was in the main house. Plenty ducks – she used to have a duck pond around here. She would help the poor, but they would have to know their place. She would have a special gate at the back that they could come in and she would give them "fritters and cocoa tea" because they are poor people, they have nothing.'

We walked through the compound and some of the women stood, and kind of bowed. Ethlyn struggled to suppress a sudden flood of emotion. Jo offered her a tissue and she smiled through the tears, eventually laughing at her own 'old woman foolishness'.

'Her neighbours – they live good in those days – would walk through the gate and get into Septimus Street, all right. I remember when we used to have inoculation, vaccination, and my mother didn't want us to have it, because in those days, you have vaccination, you get cripple up and t'ing. When the nurses come in this way, we would always go through the fence.' Ethlyn laughed at the recollection. Her laughter died down and then started up almost immediately again. It was the most I had ever heard her laugh in thirty-five years. 'They couldn't catch us. Hahahahah! We weren't in Penn Street anymore! We were in Septimus Street.'

Penn Street was light years away from the Palace Theatre, where Ethlyn wanted to go next. It was here in 1928 that Ethlyn's father went backstage to meet her mother, Pauline Fredrickson for the first time. A sand-brown, art deco building, the Palace Theatre was still standing. Posters announced a forthcoming Hollywood blockbuster; in 1928 the billboards were given over to a young all-singing, all-dancing group, 'The Butterfly Troupe'. Ethlyn's mother, just back from Broadway in New York, had top billing.

'It was really lovely, because after the cinema they would have advertised the show that's coming and they would say that "Pauline Fredrickson, late of New York, will be appearing at the Palace Theatre". I can remember one particular song: it was about the four-leaf clover.' Ethlyn laughed, shook her head and slowly began to sing, recalling the lyrics. She smiled as the words dribbled into a hum.

'It must have been corrugated cardboard, and they cut out a four-leaf clover. And I'm assuming it was tissue paper over it, and there was a hole in the middle. The younger girls put their heads through the hole, and my mother was the lead.'

It was whilst her family was living at Jones Town in 1939 that a violent rebellion broke out on the island. 'The poor people were in that mood, protesting on the streets, making their points known and heard. I remember that time, my father was a constable and in those days you had white English police chiefs. And he told us that in confronting the protestors, the commanders had ordered, "Shoot and shoot to kill."' I asked if her father had obeyed the instruction. 'That's not a nice question, Colin. Not a nice question.'

Vivian Adams was a lucky man. He'd joined the Colonial Constabulary at a time when new currents had begun blowing through the island calling for change. No black policemen had ever risen above the rank of sergeant; the constabulary needed one now, and it was Vivian's good fortune that he was black enough, but not 'too black'. Claude McKay the poet and for-mer policeman, a decade before Adams, wrote in the preface to *Constab Ballads* about his decision to quit the force: 'It is my misfortune to have a most improper sympathy with wrong-doers. I therefore never "made cases," but turning, like Nelson, a blind eye to what it was my manifest duty to see, tried to make peace, which seemed to me better.'

Corporal (eventually to become Inspector) Adams was never constituted to turn a blind eye or to make peace. Whilst his steadfast sense of duty won him praise and promotion from his police superiors, it vexed local people. As levels of violence rose in and around Jones Town, Adams requested, and was granted, a transfer to a less hazardous posting on the outskirts of Kingston, to a place called Gordon Town.

We drove up into the hills, east of Kingston, away from the dried mud and concrete empire of dust that was Jones Town, to the fecund landscape of Gordon Town where Ethlyn had lived as a teenager. In the 1940s even the hills of Gordon Town were scarred by these turbulent times. In one incident, 'Black Saturday', a riotous crowd surrounded the police station intending to burn it to the ground. Ethlyn's father faced them down with his service revolver. A few hundred yards from the station, the family rented a house called 'Enfield'.

'It was exciting for us. Well, to begin with, my father had to get a horse to go in the mountains to visit the people and to do his work. He was in charge of all this area.'

'Did the horse have a name?'

'Caesar. His name was Caesar. He had a stable man. We call him Jim Breeze.'

Ethlyn hurried along as if on stepping-stones that were in danger of disappearing. Gordon Town had a lush, verdant beauty. The fresh air, all the more welcome after the fumes from car jams of Kingston, was sweet. A stillness belied the sound of a stream rushing down below in the ravine and the non-stop chirping of cicadas. Elsewhere, little pigs roamed and foraged in thinning bushes. Foliage was pared back where vigilant locals had taken cutlasses to it. But the leaves and branches at the tops of tall trees kissed and canopied the road. We were safe and far removed from the ever-present threat of downtown.

'It looks like this might be the place.' Ethlyn pressed nervously on the buzzer on the gate of a well-maintained property. It looked new and luxurious, but not exclusive, with a huge lignum vitae veranda, wooden shutters and walls painted lime-green.

'Plenty mosquitoes up here,' she whispered. A slim and sprightly sixty-something-year-old man, his skin as dark and shiny as the veranda, appeared from around the side of the house. He put a rake to one side, pressed a button and the gate slid slowly open. I introduced myself, aware that I spoke too quickly, but to have slowed down would have seemed patronising. I needed to repeat myself three times before the man, a gardener, gained some semblance of what I was saying.

'Your muma leave Jamaica thirty-five, forty years ago?' He smiled, 'And she jus' come back now? She lose her way? This your mother?' He removed his hat. 'Evening Mrs.'

I recounted how Ethlyn's father had been a policeman responsible for the area. The man was silent in the way I was familiar with Jamaicans; they held their silence until they were sure.

'So, we are looking for the house that she used to live in, and we believe this is the one.'

'What is the name?' He asked.

'Enfield,' answered Ethlyn. 'Duvall used to own it. I used to know his son – Donald.'

'Mus here sah,' said the gardener. 'Yesss, Councillor Duvall.'

'That's the one,' Ethlyn beamed. The light was beginning to fade, but she sparkled. 'Donald Duvall, that's the one.'

'Teddy Duvall's son. Yes, right here. This Ted house.'

'They had . . . my father had, I think it was an African, name Jim Breeze. You ever hear anything about Jim Breeze?'

'Jim Breeze,' a smile crept along the gardener's face until his whole face, every inch, was smiling. '. . . mi gran-uncle.'

'Whaaa! All right, all right. Hey hey,' Ethlyn whooped. 'What you saying?'

'My gran-uncle,' he said slowly and, by way of confirmation added, 'My grandmother brother.'

'Jim Breeze, him dead is he?' The gardener nodded, and taking in his acknowledgement Ethlyn continued. 'He used to look after my father horse for him, you know.'

'Nice nice, nice . . . I am McGann.'

'That's right. It was four brothers come up to this bush place. Duvalls, McGann, I think it was Showter and I don't remember what the other one was.'

'Yes, it's here I born and go back and spend a little time in town you know. I come back here in seventy-seven. I come back up here to live.'

Every time McGann spoke, Ethlyn exclaimed 'All right.' It had the same sound and characteristic of the 'Amens' that rang out from Dale Road when one of the church elders testified.

'Well, here more cooler, more steadier, you know and all those kind of things.'

'All right.'

'Yeah, you know town rough because if you were to live in town now, every likkle t'ing . . . bwoi . . . town rough, town rough. 'Cause up here maybe you can plant one piece of yam, cassava and coco – any likkle t'ing when you nah have the cash money. Sometimes you can draw a likkle cut of callaloo, all dem kinda t'ing.'

'All right.'

'But inna town you can't do that.'

'You know what's exciting?' My mother pointed through the trees towards the sound of rushing water. 'Going down the river and setting your fish pot to catch the janga, when river come down.'

'True, true, true, true.'

'We always go up in the hill and get spring water.'

I couldn't locate what was odd, what had changed about my mum. And then I realised what it was. Of course, my mum was flirting with McGann. I had never, not once throughout my childhood and early adulthood, thought of her as a sexual being. But here she was now, charming and alluring, filling the air with excitement. Her good humour was infectious; Enfield was magical, and nobody wanted to be the one to announce that now might be the time to leave before it got dark.

When McGann offered, 'You want to come inside and take a look around?' it broke the spell. Some sudden propriety returned to Ethlyn who, declining McGann's offer, bid a gracious farewell.

I had never heard her talk before of the Duvalls, and walking down the hill away from Enfield, I wanted to know more, as the son, Donald Duvall, had evidently been keen on her.

'Yes, and his father wanted me to marry him and said that ring would be the most expensive ring in Jamaica. That engagement ring.'

'But that didn't tempt you?'

'No, I was too glamorous.' Her tone was wistful. 'I thought I had better opportunities than that.'

'So, you spurned him? But I don't understand. Why?'

Ethlyn wasn't prepared to answer directly. I knew better than to push her once she'd made her mind up, but by way of an explanation, she told me the story of her father's admonition when she grew old enough to start having boy-friends. Vivian took his daughter to the dining room and tapped on the sandalwood table. 'Nothing darker than that. I don't want you bringing anyone to this house darker than that.'

'Ahh, so Donald Duvall was too dark?'

Ethlyn didn't answer, but I held out for an answer, at least, as to what happened to him – who he eventually married.

'Imagine if you had married him. You'd have lived up in the big house instead of the poky few rooms in Farley Hill; you'd have had the biggest ring on the island.'

'What about the mosquitoes?' said Ethlyn. 'I can't see me living up in this bush place with all these mosquitoes. I was always stubborn. What is in you is in you.' She refused to indulge my fantasy.

Regaining her good cheer, she looked over her shoulder, turned back and whispered: 'We better leave before Donald come back. It wouldn't be fair on him. I don't want him to get any ideas in my old age.'

Ethlyn's stories seemed like ancient fables, but they'd only occurred thirty or forty years previously, yesterday really. We were all sad to leave that enchanted place.

Growing up in Luton in the 1960s and 70s, I always knew my mother was a snob. She would not have denied it, but I never understood how that could be so. We lived in a run-down council house on an impoverished estate; she worked as a machinist at a factory, on the production line at Vauxhall Motors; we lived hand-to-mouth on credit and feared its refusal. Yet here, in Jamaica, I could begin to comprehend how she might still have felt a cut above her neighbours in Farley Hill, the equivalent of the poor people of Jones Town whom Granny Reid was happy to help out, so long as they knew their place. The English people on the estate had the backing of centuries of Empire, with an imagined civilising mission behind them, and yet they boiled their knickers in the same pots they used to boil their potatoes; they spat into their drinking glasses to give them a shine. And Ethlyn would bemoan the fact of the tragedy that had befallen her to live in their midst. After all, back in Jamaica, she lamented, 'I never put basket 'pon my head go market.'

'Then what your name?'
  'Ethlyn.'
  'Where you live?'
  'I live in England.'
  'Ahhh. Mi can't see ya know,' said Uncle Wesley. 'Mi have glaucoma.'

Many of Ethlyn's family emigrated like her; some to England, others to Canada and the USA, but her uncle Wesley never left the island. She hadn't seen him in forty years, and it was with some trepidation that we'd come to the suburbs of Kingston to meet him. 'My father, Vivian, didn't treat him good; he was actually ashamed of him,' whispered Ethlyn as we got out of the car and approached his home. 'My father said he wouldn't amount to anything.'

Wesley was a small man with fine hair and soft skin. He was retired, in his late seventies and used to work as a barber, but now, he told us, he was blind. If he'd never amounted to anything, then someone must have forgotten to tell the trio of women who fussed over and attended to him. Their extraordinary tenderness did not appear to be put on for our benefit. Wesley had recently had a shower and, sitting at a table in a simple string vest and trousers with the legs rolled up, one of the women oiled and massaged his bare skin whilst the others prepared food for his visitors. Apart from giving us their names, the women never volunteered how they were associated with Wesley.

My mother held her uncle's hand as they spoke.

'So you have more sisters so?'

'How many of we now?' My mum for some reason looked to me to help her. Counting them on her fingers, she answered, laughing at her own temporary forgetfulness. 'Three: Monique, Sheila and Amy. Amy in America.'

'Ohh, den brother Viv did have plenty of you?'

'Yes, you remember the boys. You know Elden, Victor, Ramon, then there was me, Amy, Bertram, Sheila, Castus, Percy and Monique. Just ten of us. Two died – yes, Sitting Bull was Vivian too but Sitting Bull died.'

'Him name Sitting Bull? What kind of a name that? Him real name Sitting Bull?'

'No, he looked like an Indian Chief. You know Indian Chief, Sitting Bull; straight hair, fair, and just scowl like the Indian, you know what I mean? Wouldn't smile. So they call . . . my father pet name . . . you know, Sitting Bull.'

'And what he die from?'

'Well, bad care.' Ethlyn lowered her voice, until it was almost confessional: 'The midwife came, in those days, the midwife delivered the baby at home. Well she brought a trainee nurse with her.'

Uncle Wesley, listening intensely, interrupted: 'Inna England?'

'No man,' said Ethlyn. 'Jamaica. And I'm assuming that some infection got on the navel. The navel wouldn't heal, and then when it gone too bad now, someone said to put cornmeal poultice, but too late. "Oh dear," my father said to the police-man where we were living, "JT, my baby is going." It's terrible you know.'

It was noticeable that there'd been few references to Vivian or Doc Saunders from their brother, Wesley, and he hadn't enquired after them. When I asked Ethlyn about the silence, she shook her head: 'Bad blood. Too much bad blood in this family. I'm glad we come look for him though.'

Wesley had been ostracised by the Adamses when they were still in Jamaica, and Ethlyn wondered now why she had ever gone along with it. Up until our visit, other than his 'good hair', I'd never heard anyone in the family speak about the old man. We were in the last few days of the trip, and Ethlyn had become increasingly reflective. Each night now, before bed, we sat and talked through the events of the day and plotted ahead for the day to come. My mum had surprised herself with the significance she attached to the brief stop, no more than a pit stop really, with her uncle. Even if all she got from the visit was a chance to see the old man and repair the breach, it would have been worth it. 'It wasn't much, but it was something.'

Mandeville was the number one destination for those 'gone-to-foreign' Jamaicans in Britain who had decided to return 'home'. We'd arranged for Mandeville to be the last leg of our venture. It was home to Yvonne, Ethlyn's cousin, who ran the popular store, 'Sinclair's Bargain Centre', in town. The store's title did not disguise anything; it had zero pretensions. Its TV advert simply spelled out: 'We sell SHOES'. It was a strange bargain-basement establishment for someone like Yvonne to run. She had spent most of her adult life in Miami and touted, in ways she could no longer discern herself, her metropolitan pretensions. She was only a cousin, but Ethlyn thought of her as a glamorous older sister.

Born in Jamaica, Yvonne had only returned to the island in the previous year with her adult daughter, Michelle. Whilst Yvonne slotted right back into the raw challenges posed by facety Jamaicans, Michelle seemed permanently bemused by them, especially by their directness. 'Fat gal, how come you so big and nice and sexy?' scrawny young men would enquire of the six-foot Michelle. There was really no answer to that, no matter how long you thought about it.

For good measure, Yvonne was delightfully rude about her compatriots, but she reserved her scorn and verbal artillery for the biggest sinners: the British returnees. They bought properties in gated communities, were petrified when they went to bed of being chopped up by burglars, and played endless VHS cassettes of old British TV comedies.

Ethlyn's cousin saw no irony in the manner in which she replicated Miami in her own home. She spoke with a heavy, theatrical North American twang. A satellite dish connected her with the mainland. There was no way we could come to her yard without being given a tour of all of the channels on offer before settling down to watch *Once Upon a Time in America*. I was relieved when power cuts interrupted the viewing; Yvonne was far more entertaining. She was loose and languorous. When she kicked off her shoes, I would not have been surprised had she asked me to massage her feet, and I would not have declined.

Yvonne was both sizzle and steak, and in the morning as we prepared our bags, she barred the door and would only make way when Ethlyn promised, as Yvonne demanded, that not only would she come back and relocate to Jamaica but that she would be their permanent guest. She meant it, too, and I could see that perhaps for the first time, outside of all the bluster and joking, Ethlyn was seriously considering it.

Before leaving Mandeville, there'd been talk of us looking up Mona, an old West Indian church friend from Luton who'd retired and relocated to the area. Yvonne knew Mona and had joked about her English pretension, common among the returnees, of tiresomely complaining of the cold, and wearing long stockings, and, in the height of the Jamaican summer, insisting on taking tea in the afternoon. Listening to Ethlyn hoot with delight, it was apparent that something had shifted in my mother's mindset during her time with Yvonne; an old snobbishness or sense of her middle-class status, partially suppressed back in Luton, had fully resurfaced.

As we approached Mona's house, Ethlyn became increasingly agitated and was finally adamant that we should not slow down; we should drive on by. When I asked her why she'd changed her mind, Ethlyn recounted how Mona had insulted her twenty years ago. One hectic Saturday afternoon in the 70s, the house money, as usual, had been borrowed back by Bageye for a bet (a sure-fire win) on the horses. 'But the horse didn't even place.' Ethlyn snorted back her derision at the memory. There was no food in the house and Ethlyn had gone to borrow some money from Mona, but 'all that woman give me was a bag of sugar.' From that day Ethlyn had stopped speaking to Mona.

We'd turned off the main road to find Mona's place but my mum commanded me now to wheel and come again. In answer to my look of bewilderment and disappointment she answered: 'My spirit just can't take that woman.'

Mandeville was just seventy miles from Montego Bay, but the roads were bad; it would take us four hours. Perhaps half-way along, we came to a huge roundabout, marked by the unsettling distinction of having no route signs for any of its five exits. Thankfully, there was little traffic. I circumnavigated the roundabout three times, none the wiser, before pulling over onto some rough ground, close to a wooden shack selling soft drinks and snacks. No sooner had I turned off the engine than twenty or so women, who'd been shading under trees from the punishing sun, ran towards and swarmed around the car. 'Hmm mmh,' said Ethlyn. 'Ah wha' this now?'

Each of the middle-aged women carried what looked like a plastic washing-up bowl. Inside each bowl was the same thing: dozens of crayfish. Crying out the price and lowering it every time a competitor bettered them, they pushed, shoved, and cursed, trying to squeeze the bowls into the gap of the closing car window. I only stopped winding up the window when I feared trapping one of their hands. Still they jostled to get close. Some also tried the passenger-side window. Ethlyn sadly shook her head. There was no possibility of buying crayfish from one of the women without buying from them all; it was best that all were left unhappy. We sat in the chilled, air-conditioned interior whilst the women continued to pound on the windows and plead to be chosen.

Perhaps after five minutes, maybe more, only when it became clear that there would be no purchase from the wealthy tourists, did they drift away, back out of the sun towards the shade of the trees, awaiting the next car to come along on the near-deserted road. If my mother, Jo or Chris felt as ashamed as me, then they judged now was not the time to say. We exited the car and headed towards the shack.

We queued, thirsty, hungry and still not fully emerged from the shock of the encounter with the crayfish sellers. While we were wrestling with the labels and brands of the unfamiliar-looking soft drinks on the shelves of the shack, I distinctly heard the sound of someone calling my mother's name.

'Sister Grant? Oh my, Sister Grant. Is that you?'

We turned round to see Brother Williams, the man who'd made it his mission to personally deliver *The Gleaner* to our house all those years ago, beaming at us.

'I thought it was you.'

'Praise God,' Ethlyn exclaimed. 'Brother Williams! I heard you had come back. Oh, this is a blessing, a real, real blessing. Where's Sister Williams?'

Brother Williams gestured towards a tree. His wife stood beside their van, trying to shade from the sun. She didn't move from her spot, but simply waved and smiled.

'Oh it's a blessing,' my mum repeated and, turning to me, added, 'And still you doubt?' This was no chance meeting; it was a sign. God was sending a message. Didn't I understand? I did not and, backing out of the conversation, I left them to it, talking some old-time talk.

'Oh surely, I do love Jamaica. This is just where I was born and I'm feeling so proud to be back home in Middle Quarters. In fact, if you notice, I've gone a bit slim 'cause, I'm working pretty hard planting sugar cane and anything that I can find, and in fact, the sun is so hot that I sweat quite a lot.'

Ethlyn asked him about the coincidence, wondering what he was doing milling around Middle Quarters.

'Well umm, it's funny about it . . . that ahhh Sister Williams, she wanted to come down to the square here to do a little selling you know. She had some clothes that she would like to sell and so we come along today and it was really a surprise, and I think it was a good day.'

We chatted for another half hour and then continued on our way. Ethlyn seemed buoyed by the meeting of Sister and Brother Williams, but I couldn't rid myself of the thought that if we were to return in a few years, we'd find that the Williamses had joined the higglers with their bowls of crayfish. I kept such thoughts to myself and asked my mum what she felt having seen them.

'Coming down the road here, look at all these houses that

people from England are building up now. Everybody is coming home after you reach sixty-plus. Everybody wants to come home because it's nice here. Ahhh . . . I can't wait. I'm looking at the land already, what I'm going to buy. I have a dream: I'm coming home.'

Ethlyn didn't speak again till we arrived at the airport and even then, her speech was perfunctory. It was disturbing; she reminded me of someone with bipolar disorder who suddenly comes down when the mood-regulating drugs take effect. As we passed through the departure gates to get back on board to go to England, she flopped down at the first available seat; she could not go on.

'I'm upset, but what can I do? I have to have my cry. I cry because I'm so upset, I'm shaking. No matter how poor or what problem or whatever it is, home is home. Going back now is sad.'

'So, are you not looking forward to arriving back in England?' I said fearing I, too, would start to cry.

'To be honest . . . no. There's not much fond memories of England, we've got to be honest with ourselves, you know. Not much happiness, really; real happiness . . . no.' Ethlyn confessed that she'd already asked Yvonne to look about getting some land. She foresaw building a nice house and living happily in it. 'I'll visit England to see you and your children,' she said. 'But to live again? No.'

All that was long ago. My mother was in her early sixties then; she's ninety now. But her homecoming, heralded by our two-week recce, was not permanent; the little bit of Jamaican land she had her eye on remained unpurchased; her retirement home in the sun was never built. She did make a decision to move – not across the Atlantic, but to Brighton – just one hundred miles from Luton, to be closer to me and her grand-children. It was not, as expected, the culmination of a romantic notion driven by a dream, but a prudent one. Jamaica is a dangerous place. I do love the island but it is no country for old-timers, especially ones like my mother who'd have spurned the sadly sensible trend of returnees shutting themselves off safely from burglars and gunmen, in gated communities.

Sometimes I wake up from reveries of that 1990s trip and I tell myself that Ethlyn realised her dream; that my mother never ever was thwarted; that she danced with Anne Hegarty when her would-be partner proved less than gallant at St Columba's College; that she restarted her correspondence with Councillor Duvall's son and that she found a perfect plot of land, built a comfortable home and returned to Jamaica. That's what I tell myself.

Charlie

You have fi have love songs

Ethlyn's past had always intrigued me, especially when I saw aspects of my own character and code reflected in her. My mother's youthful hesitancy over aligning herself with Councillor Duvall's son did not ring true to her explanation. 'I thought I was better than that; I was really something to look at,' she had said. But I saw her spurning of Donald Duvall as a nervous rejection of intimacy as much as an adherence to some family code of not marrying beneath yourself, or saddling yourself with someone whose skin was too dark. I would not have been vocal but I, too, as a young adult had complied, silently, with a family code when it came to romance. Even at medical school, which I began in fulfilment of a family prophecy in 1981, I wasn't ready for intimacy. In any case, all the female students were white. Romantic relationships were a conundrum, an inversion of my mother's dilemma. She, as a nineteen-year-old, had feared any partner who was 'too black', but when I was nineteen the idea of dating a *white* woman was unconscionable. In my head, I waged a solitary, cultural and racial war that would have been oblivious to my peers; though I convinced myself that an occasional game of squash with students such as Sibylla, Sian or Glynis, or a trip to the West End to catch a discounted theatre show with one of them, fell short of betraying the race.

Until one day, I overheard Glynis with three or four of her friends say, with a distinct and faintly humorous question in her voice, 'I think I'm going out with Colin Grant!' Well, that put paid to that! I ensured the mistaken impression was never given again.

Nonetheless, there was one student who gave me pause to consider the primacy of loyalty to family and race over a confused and yearning heart. That student was Charlie who, but for the colour of her skin, was, in my imagination, black.

The brightest room in 'The London', our teaching hospital in the East End, was reserved for the dead, the cadavers awaiting dissection. The living had to make do with the half-light of the building's dark interior. The medical school was attached to the hospital, a bleak-looking building which resembled a Victorian workhouse. Thick grey grime covered its brick walls from years of exposure to fumes from the traffic that clogged the neighbouring streets. The London appeared to be permanently girded by a cloud, but it was even gloomier inside.

Heavy wooden doors, which remained mostly closed, and wood-panelled walls lined with black-and-white photos of austere physicians in stiff suits, sprouting even more stiff nineteenth-century moustaches and beards, seemed designed to underscore the serious business undertaken at the school. The central stairway, though, ascended towards the light, let in by a glass roof at the top of the building, four flights up, where the cadavers were housed in the dissection room.

'Dab some camphor oil under your nose,' I was advised by a student in the year above, 'and for God's sake, don't have any breakfast before you go in.' I arrived at The London with half an hour to spare. But no matter how early I got there, the female students were bound to have pipped me; they were always more demonstrably keen and conscientious. Sure enough, on entering the courtyard leading to the medical school, I spied Charlie ahead of me.

She was a natural-born advocate with a fierce determination to call out injustice whenever she saw it. If you wanted to find her out of college time, the radical bookshop on Whitechapel High Street was always a good bet. Apart from pencilled-in eyebrows, Charlie never wore make-up. She sported a pair of dungarees, and a signature beret, which she never seemed to take off, covered her shaved head. I always loved the way she walked around the college grounds, wreathed in an intelligent sadness that you dared not interrupt. And I was thrilled to have somehow caught Charlie's attention over the last few months, to have been chosen as her friend. I didn't realise until much later, that as far as she was concerned, I'd been auditioning for the part.

Before joining The London I'd only ever had one girlfriend: Nicole. Because she was half Greek, I convinced myself that I wasn't selling out the race and betraying other possible black girlfriends by dating her. But I had finished with Nicole, sacrificed her, in my desire not to be distracted from the mission of getting into medical school. I never told Charlie but, of all the female students (there were no black women in sight), she was the closest I'd get to a black woman; she was a soul sister. Maybe she could be more than a soul sister, but college was too intimate and exposing to think of courting her in that way. And of course, it was presumptuous. She was Charlie, for Christ's sake; she'd already shown her disdain for boys whose testosterone clouded their judgement.

I followed Charlie into the building and up the steps to the dissection room, but kept my distance. Dozens of students were already there.

It was the autumn of 1981, our second month on the course, and we, the latest intake of nineteen-year-old medical students, were instructed to assemble outside of the dissection room in preparation for our first lesson in anatomy.

A technician in a yellowing-white lab coat greeted us. Mr Quinn's putty-like skin needed to have seen more sunlight over the years; and I would not like to have been the comb that passed through that greasy, grey hair. His eyes flicked over the horde of students but he was perfectly still. He'd have waited all day if need be, adding to the drama of the enormity of what we were about to experience. We were soon to 'behold man', he told us. 'Forget Rolls Royce, Lamborghini and Ferrari; man is the ultimate machine.' The sentiment and phrase had obviously been rehearsed over many years, yet his voice was measured and sincere: think 1950s Pathé News broadcast. In a few moments we would be in the 'privileged position' of observing that which the cadavers had never witnessed when alive: their inner workings.

On Quinn's instruction we pulled open and fought our way into freshly starched white lab coats, and pocketed our instruments of learning: pristine dissection kits, scissors, tweezers and scalpels with cold, metal, detachable blades in wrap-around green cloth pouches.

The previous year I'd worked as a hospital porter – a strategic, part-time job, which, when highlighted on my CV, I'd hoped would boost my chances of getting into medical school. Though I had ferried the recently dead from hospital wards to the mortuary, and witnessed the speed with which the corpse became a lifeless shell, I had still imagined that the dissection room would be a kind of human abattoir and that we'd all be sloshing around in blood and offal.

Charlie edged ever closer to me in the countdown to entering the room. She was pale and prone to blushing, but it was she who asked whether I was nervous. I shook my head.

'Not even a little? Well, just remember . . .' she raised a fist and flexed her biceps, 'I'm here to protect you.'

I didn't really know how to reply. Charlie had a kind of teasing humour, sometimes dark, that was always difficult to understand. And anyway, what did I know? All I really knew was how to pass exams.

The students moved solemnly towards the swing doors of the dissection room like churchgoers rising from their pews to take Holy Communion. Charlie and I set off together. But the first step across the threshold to 'behold man' was not as shocking as the feeling of Charlie's tremulous hand that had slipped discreetly into mine.

Even in the short time we'd known each other, Charlie had emerged as someone who was more a protector than needed to be protected. She'd berate me for my passivity when lecturers strayed close to the borders of offence. Walvin was the biggest culprit.

'Why are young black men six times more likely to be diagnosed with schizophrenia?' Dr Walvin ranged across the Athenaeum lecture hall, tall and imperious. No one answered. Even after two months we were still struggling to read Walvin's prickliness; to work out how to navigate it. He'd a titanic temper, complicated by a slight stutter, which resulted in a torrent of verbal ejaculation when riled.

'Six times more likely!' Walvin was a provocateur. The tangy sarcasm of his voice, I suspected, had not lessened in all the years of lecturing. His intellect was obviously wasted on medical students; but, God help him, he enjoyed teaching. He had a talent for it. Walvin reached inside the breast-pocket of his white overcoat and extracted what looked like a silver telescopic aerial that formerly must have been attached to a transistor radio. Now adapted as a pointer, one that appeared to have a life of its own, veering from side to side, it came to rest, unmistakably pointing at me. Walvin seemed faintly irritated by my silence. Given my complexion, surely I must have a view on the matter? His laser gaze drilled all the way through to the back of my head. 'Why do you . . .' He left a gap for me to declare my name.

'Grant.'

'Why do you, Grant, have a greater chance of being diagnosed as schizophrenic than any other medical student in this room, hmm?' He was as patient as a priest awaiting details of a confession. There was not a murmur from the class, but then it was only our second month at medical school; there were no ties that bound us, other than fear of personal exposure and humiliation. My only recourse was to pretend it wasn't happening to me. I was no different from the others; I wouldn't even leap to my own defence.

Charlie, who'd been mumbling under her breath, thrust her hand in the air. Walvin pointed at her to go ahead.

'Why are you asking him?' She asked.

'Why do you think?' Walvin responded.

'It doesn't seem fair.'

'Fair? This isn't a nursery, my dear. The world is as it is and you'd do well to pay attention.'

Charlie fidgeted and fumed. When it was clear that no matter how long he stared at her, there'd be no further response, Walvin turned away from her and addressed the whole room: 'Because black people are schooled in paranoia.'

I was stunned and offended; but his insight was surprising. Usually, Walvin seemed determined to provoke; here, though, there was an element of truth – even sympathy – in his assertion. He scowled at the back row from where, now that the tension had lessened, one or two titters emerged. The higher incidence wasn't specific to black people, of course, but to all migrants, he wanted us to know. In fact, the Norwegian population of Milwaukee, he intoned, exceeded all groups in percentage of schizophrenics – a fact which produced another flurry of tittering. When the room had sufficiently calmed again, he came to the main point, the lesson that we were to take away from this, only our second lecture from him: 'Think pathology!' Walvin collapsed the aerial, slipped it back into his pocket, before continuing: 'You're walking down Brick Lane and you see a Bengali woman with a hacking cough, honking onto the pavement. Observe the colour of her sputum. Is there blood in it? Tuberculosis? What about the West Indian tramp who cannot pass a cigarette butt on Whitechapel High Street without pocketing it? Obsessive compulsive? Or something else? Perhaps the butt is a form of currency. Where's he likely to have been? Anyone? Anyone seen him?' Walvin could not resist one last attempt to draw me in: 'I know you've seen him.' I shook my head, perhaps a little too strenuously.

'You're not under oath!' Walvin laughed. 'You presumably will not think it unreasonable to suggest that a black man walks down the street with a heightened perception of other blacks. No more than the fact that the driver of a Porsche notices all other Porsches before the Ford Escort – whatever that is. Or, or that the sufferer of postpartum depression, pushing her neonate in a pram, is suddenly aware of all the other perambulators she had been blind to prior to her pregnancy. Do I go on? Am I being unreasonable? Not, do I go on? But, do I *go on*? I have been known to.' He was beginning to enjoy his fiendishly clever self. I tried not to blink. I told myself that if I blinked, Walvin would not stop.

'Well stranger or not,' Dr Walvin continued, walking up the stairs of the lecture hall dividing the group, 'it will be your job to pay attention to the pathology all around you.' Walvin straightened himself. If he'd been an eagle, his wings would have stretched to their fullest: 'Do not squander your time here. There is much to learn over the coming years. Keep your eyes peeled and "think pathology".'

Dr Walvin probably didn't realise that, in my case, he was preaching to the converted. Aged nineteen, I'd already begun to school myself in unfeeling. Emotions were overrated, and for reasons that now seem unfathomable but appeared worthy at the time, I'd decided to heed Bageye's warning never to reveal to 'the man' what you were truly thinking. At home we'd been schooled not to engage, and here Walvin was encouraging much the same. We were always to 'think pathology'. We were not to think emotionally of people on the streets of Whitechapel; they were just walking pathology, awaiting a diagnosis.

LESSON 1: Identify in the cadaver the bony landmarks of the thorax, clavicle and suprasternal (jugular) notch, manubrium and body of the sternum.

When the swing doors flapped open, we were exposed immediately to the blindingly brilliant white-tiled walls of the dissection room, to its cathedral-like high ceiling with a glass roof. The walls were flanked by several stainless steel tanks; skeletons were hanging from what looked like coat rails and there were glass jars with bewildering specimens of deformed foetuses, brains, livers and other viscera. The smell was nauseating – the acrid smell of formaldehyde in the dissection room was overwhelming.

After the orderly procession filed into the room, there was a bit of a staggered dash for the dissection tables. Staggered, because many students hedged their bets and waited to see which table the two inseparable Sarahs, who'd already been identified as the year's geniuses, were heading for.

We spread out as we moved through the room and peeled off to station ourselves, six per dissection table, alongside a cadaver. It took perhaps ten minutes before the configurations of students-to-cadavers were settled. After all, we barely knew each other, and were not only choosing whom to dissect but also our accomplices for the year it would take to reveal, with scissors, scalpels and saws, the full anatomy of the deceased.

Finally, our eyes rested on the twenty tables with twenty bodies in two rows – a pitiful, silent population lying dutifully on dissection tables, waiting for whatever was going to happen to them. Each cadaver was covered with a white plastic sheet, and there was a stainless steel bucket under every table. The sheets were pulled back. I can still see the faces of the dead people; their mouths were open. I had expected to see bodies racked in agony: they were not. Their faces had been shaved; all of the hair had been removed from their heads, armpits and genitals; but stubble still sprouted from the chins of the men.

Charlie and I wandered over to an incomplete group in need of a couple more students, listening to a youthful, bow-tie-wearing anatomist enjoining them to respect the fact that the cadaver – whom they were arranged either side of – had once been a man. I thought of the death of Che Guevara – the newspaper photo of the half-bored, half-excited Bolivian soldiers mocking the corpse of the executed revolutionary. The anatomist's entreaties had been unnecessary. We remained silent and shocked, like dumbstruck relatives at the graveside where the coffin was yet to be lowered into the ground. Almost immediately, after the anatomist had departed to counsel another table, some wag started calling the cadaver Mr Flint, and the name stuck.

Mr Flint was stiff and solid. The blood had been drained from the corpse and the skin impregnated with embalming fluids so that it resembled dimpled orange peel. There was a grey hue to his skin that we were reluctant to touch. Looking back now, it seems odd that our first interaction with a patient would be with the deceased. But in order to dissect Mr Flint we would need, at some level, to stop thinking of him as human; to consider he'd formerly been just walking pathology, to recognise that the subject had become an object; that his corpse had become a cadaver. Nobody in our group, though, was keen to lay a finger, never mind a hand, on Mr Flint; he intrigued but also repulsed us.

'So who's going to make the first cut?' asked the wag, who was definitely not going to volunteer.

After a minute or two, Charlie nudged me and I unfurled my dissection kit, selected the scalpel and snapped a new blade into position. I placed the tip of the scalpel at Mr Flint's throat, but I couldn't push down and penetrate the skin; it seemed wrong, aesthetically and morally. I hesitated, unsure how to proceed but too embarrassed to give up. Another hand, a gloved one, took the scalpel and unsteadily pressed and pulled down and into his skin, just below his Adams' apple. 'It's not so bad,' said Charlie, handing the scalpel back to me. 'You'll get used to it.'

The London was famously associated with Joseph Merrick, the Elephant Man. To my mind, something of the Victorian gloom of that period, during which Merrick had been rescued from a human zoo and brought to The London, still shrouded the building brimming with sick, but hopeful people who for generations had surrendered their bodies to the medical school, having their pathologies put on display for the education of the students. That was the unwritten contract forged between medics and patients. In fact, the gnarled and twisted bones of the Elephant Man were still to be found in the medical school's museum. Other colleges such as UCH and Barts may have been located in more glamorous settings, but we at The London had our pick of spectacular, suppurating diseases: crude and cruel maladies; the most pustulant sores; neglected disfigurements and myriad end-stage conditions more commonly associated with Merrick's time.

Nothing bad had ever happened to the senior house officer, Mike Clifford, and nothing bad was ever likely to happen to him. If it did then it would be chalked up as a divine intervention and test of his faith. He even saw the uncorrected squint in his left eye as a 'blessing'. I envied his approach to life: unencumbered by complications. A handful of students joined us – me, Charlie and others from our year – on his junior ward round.

Clifford beckoned us to follow him. 'I've something to show you,' he enthused. We struggled to keep up as he chased after his own excitement, preceding him down the obstetrics and gynaecology ward. We assembled at a bed bordered by three screens of pleated curtains on trolley wheels. Clifford pulled back one of the screens.

A young black girl, perhaps seventeen years old, with ribbons in her plaited hair, lay in bed with the sheets pulled up to her chin. I determined not to place any significance on her colour, nor to signal the subtle black salute. Whatever was coming, I did not want her to be black. Why did she have to be black? Clifford explained who we were; asked 'do you mind?' and without waiting for an answer proceeded to gently peel the sheets from her; though he paused every so often, to check it was still OK. He stopped when the sheets were just above her knees. The girl wasn't wearing knickers. Exposed to the air, heat surged from her lower body. I cannot say whether she was embarrassed because like all of the students I wasn't observing her face. We stared at her vagina, at the cluster of vaginal warts that had begun to sprout like fungi from the base of a tree.

The senior house officer canvassed for a volunteer to conduct an examination of the girl. It was noticeable that he asked without conviction. He reached for a box of surgical gloves beside the bed. Though like everybody else I had backed away, when he turned around, I was the closest to him. Clifford proffered the gloves. I declined: I had no intention of touching her – anywhere.

I shook my head.

In spite of myself, my eyes fixed on the warts, which appeared to pulse the longer I stared. I didn't want to prolong her agony. I wished it could all be over, for everybody, especially for her. Would Clifford have exposed a seventeen-year-old white girl in this way? He wouldn't have understood the history that lay behind such a question. To him she wasn't a black woman or any woman at all; she was just walking pathology, an interesting case. I looked at Clifford's ugly, innocent face and said nothing, and despised myself for my cowardice.

Charlie tried to roll the sheet back up over the patient's thighs, but she brushed her hands aside.

I shrugged, more at Charlie than at Clifford or the girl, but Charlie stared at me, disappointedly, it seemed. I focused on the middle distance, walking backwards through the students, stepping on toes and clattering into the screens. Once through, I snapped back the screens into place, shutting it out, shutting it all out.

LESSON 2: Remove the intercostal muscles from the anterior halves of the first five spaces on the left.

You couldn't help but wonder what last words would have escaped Mr Flint's lips; or try to imagine, when you looked at him, who he was when he'd been alive. Peter Reid stood beside me. I whispered to him: 'What do you think he's saying?'

'He's dead,' Reid answered drily.

'You think he's saying he's dead?'

'No. He *is* dead!'

Reid was not atypical. Most students lacked imagination, whether by default or design it was hard to tell. But it certainly had practical benefits. Answering excited relatives' quests for updates about my glamorous profession, I'd complain about the narrow-minded philistinism of medical school, and they'd chastise me: 'You think too much! Just knuckle down. Do what everybody else does.' I didn't do as I was told; it didn't fit my personal constitution, nor Charlie's. That was one of the reasons why I liked her: she thought too much as well.

Quinn worked his way down the room, checking on progress at each dissection table. He stopped at the foot of our table. 'You can touch him. Go on. You're allowed,' he said. It sounded more like a command than an invitation. Quinn must have been irritated by our timidity because he added testily: 'He's already given his permission!'

We were saved by another man in a shabbier white coat who drew up alongside Quinn. Every student had heard the rumours about the fossilised older gent, a member of staff called Simpkins. Years beyond retirement age, Mr Simpkins should have been put out to graze long ago but the college hierarchy had made an exception and allowed him to continue to teach.

If anything, Simpkins was stiffer than Quinn. His shoulders were so rounded you might have mistaken him for a congenital hunchback, but his bearing was more likely that of a man who'd spent decades hunched over cadavers on dissection tables. You could tell by the way that Quinn took a few steps back to give the older man room that Simpkins was his superior and an actual anatomist. Quinn departed and we were left with Simpkins.

'It seems an unpleasant business, doesn't it?' said Mr Simpkins. He spoke in such a quiet, reflective voice that he might have been talking to himself. There was something likeably straightforward about him. He reminded me of the boy who when asked to describe the sea said it was 'big'. Simpkins was as old and eternal as the sea; there was no possibility of rolling back the years to reveal his youth. 'One can't escape Hunter's argument,' the old anatomist continued, referencing the revered eighteenth-century physician. 'Dissection, Hunter argued, informs the head, gives dexterity to the hand and familiarises the heart to a kind of necessary inhumanity.'

Simpkins smiled the way that bright, but kindly people do when they don't expect to be understood – not in the first instance, anyway. He called for a volunteer and Charlie, ever the seeker of new experiences, signalled that she was willing. He took her right hand by the wrist and set it down on the dead man's chest.

'How does that feel?'

'Cold,' answered Charlie.

'Anything else?'

'Leathery.'

'And what else?'

'Solid.'

'Solid? Would you say compact?'

Charlie nodded.

'Nowhere near as supple as a living body is it?' Simpkins suggested. 'Now, I want you to unroll your dissection kit; take out the scalpel.' He asked her to attach a blade, and, when that was done, to make an incision, 'straight as you can, down the middle of his chest.'

The anatomist kept up a running commentary throughout Charlie's preparations, making encouraging sounds. But she faltered at the very end: she could not cut deep enough into the skin. Simpkins looked round for another volunteer, 'a second pair of hands?' We must have appeared to him as blank as cows in a field, but he eventually settled on me.

'OK,' said Simpkins. 'Place your hand on hers.' Charlie blushed immediately. I wondered whether the others could see that I, too, blushed and that my woeful attempt at nonchalance was undermined by shakiness. I positioned my trembling hand lightly on the back of hers, hardly touching. 'Now press down and slide the handle and blade back towards you.'

The first layer of the cadaver's skin parted as smoothly as a zip on a skirt. Simpkins's smile would have outdone any mother's on observing her child's first steps. 'There you have it,' said Simpkins. 'By the way, you can let go now.' I had kept my hand on Charlie's awaiting the next instruction. The others laughed, and I immediately pulled my hand away.

The anatomist announced that he would have to move on to another table, but promised to return. Without him we floundered like awkward guests at a party who did not know each other; whose only connection was to the host. Charlie busied herself with the scalpel, cutting from what we would later identify as the suprasternal notch towards the navel. I was content to act as her assistant, working so close to her that her perfume (no make-up, but perfume was allowed) temporarily displaced the smell of formaldehyde. With the tweezers you could just about grasp and hold onto a corner of skin. Ten minutes passed before it took on the outline of a flap. It was ever so slightly annoying how attached Mr Flint was to his skin.

Up and down the room the first tentative incisions were being replicated. Faster than anticipated, it seemed we became habituated to the strangeness of the circumstances, so that conversations began to emerge, albeit under the strain of dissection – what anatomists call the 'chant of pleasant exploration'.

'Put away your *Gray's Anatomy*,' commanded Wendy Savage, 'there are better books if you want to understand female reproduction and sexuality.' First she held up a copy of Germaine Greer's *The Female Eunuch* and then she switched it with *Fear of Flying* by Erica Jong. 'These are the books for you.'

Wendy Savage was a legend at The London; the only female consultant of obstetrics and gynaecology among a team of six. The men were as terrified of her, I imagined, as older male readers were of the fantasies and the purity of the 'zipless fuck' espoused by Erica Jong's narrator. In particular, the male consultants fumed over Savage's rejection of elective Caesareans and her insistence on the possibility of vaginal delivery where and when possible. She ploughed on regardless of their censure.

I knew nothing about women and sexuality; only that put together they spelled trouble. But Savage's lectures and presentations electrified me and Charlie, especially. She scorned patriciarchal notions about the sanctity of the female body; she'd rather just have respect. Male students in sexual relationships should take nothing for granted; if, for instance, you lay down in bed with your girlfriend contemplating penetrative sex you were best to 'secure permission before entry'.

Savage, who wore Afghan waistcoats and was rumoured to have a black boyfriend, was sexy, I suppose. A couple of the more sensitive boys certainly thought so. After every encounter, particularly social ones (Savage had a habit of taking a handful of students to dinner at a Chinese restaurant in Lime-house), they giddily exchanged notes – 'I'm sure she was playing footsie under the table' or 'I got to tell her my theory of . . .' – about their proximity to her.

They were not alone in their admiration; Wendy Savage's convictions, even off-the-cuff remarks, carried weight. Once, when Charlie and I joined one of her soirées, she greeted us with, 'Ah, the alignment of the young and the beautiful.' What was she really telling us? We, well I, haven't stopped wondering about it since.

LESSON 3: Identify the internal thoracic artery about one centi-metre from the lateral border of the sternum.

Old Simpkins's gait was peculiar as it was distracting. He shuf-fled along, dipping and rising rhythmically, like a man who had one leg much shorter than the other. We tracked him as he made his way to our problematic cadaver. Charlie had frozen. She had made little progress since the initial incision. Tears unexpectedly slid slowly down her cheeks.

'It's nothing,' said Charlie.

Though she did not look up, she must have felt the question in our collective gaze.

'Probably just the formaldehyde,' someone volunteered.

'Yes probably,' said Charlie, laughing back the tears. 'It's funny, the freckles on his arm remind me of someone, that's all.' Hearing herself speak out loud, the thought started up the locomotive of tears again that threatened to overwhelm her.

Mr Simpkins reached over and gently removed the scalpel from Charlie and squeezed a handkerchief into her palm. 'Let me let you into a little secret,' whispered Mr Simpkins. It was apparent that he meant all of us and not just Charlie. Everyone leaned forward and Simpkins, with a voice that was shaky at first but grew stronger with each word, began his tale.

'Fifty, no, more than fifty years ago, I stood where you are standing now. Opposite me was another student. She was the most attractive woman I'd ever met. We worked on our cadaver, Mr Haselberry was his name, dissecting him for almost a year. At the end of the year I proposed to her.'

Mr Simpkins let loose a shy little half smile before continuing: 'Eventually, we were married. My wife was Jewish. It had been the custom in her family over many generations that marriage was arranged through a broker, a shadchan. And from that day onwards, we always considered Mr Haselberry to be our shadchan.'

Simpkins said no more. The tale had come to an end. His words lay lightly on us like fine snow that had not yet decided if it would settle.

I decided then and there that one day I'd marry Charlie. Mr Simpkins pulled back, as if lifting himself out of the silence. He positioned the scalpel at the point where Charlie had left off, and, in an extraordinarily straight line, began extending her incision before scooping deftly round the navel.

Whilst everyone concentrated on how he used the blunt end of the scalpel to expertly prise back the skin, I found a scrap of paper and quickly scribbled a note asking Charlie if I could come over to her flat later. I pushed the note into the pocket of her lab coat, firmly enough for her to be aware of what I was doing. She took out the note immediately, read it, smiled and mouthed, 'Yes'.

Heading to Charlie's flat I had to fight off the usual nimbus of anxiety. I never really understood why something I always looked forward to also filled me with a kind of dread. As was our habit, I brought along my half-skeleton (Charlie was still waiting for hers to arrive), and we tested each other on anatomy, naming the bones, starting with the humerus, identifying its grooves and notches. I loved the timbre and rhythm of her voice. Reciting the names – anatomical neck, greater tubercle, lesser tubercle, intertubercular groove (sulcus), lateral supracondylar ridge, radial fossa, capitulum – had a poetry to it.

Afterwards, I sat, watched and chatted with Charlie whilst she cooked. I realised now that despite the enforced gravitas of medical school, everyone in our year, with the exception possibly of Charlie, was pretty immature. After my stay at Doc Saunders's, I'd moved into a household of medics. None of us, having taken the first tentative steps on the road to a caring profession, could be counted on to pay attention to anyone other than ourselves. Jeremy, a sardonic, curly haired Anglo-Egyptian, often vexed for being mistaken as a Jew, had sad, hooded eyes and professed to want to be an air steward rather than a medic. Peter wore roll-neck jumpers, pretended to like jazz, and enjoyed ridiculing others from behind his fully grown-up beard. Annabel stored half-empty bottles of vodka under her bed. Kevin, the most joyful, would go off clubbing, announcing: 'Let's get hoolied,' but was having trouble extracting himself from the unsettling attentions of an obsessive nurse. Everyone was bluffing – including me.

I would have been happy to never set foot in the dissection room again. I didn't want to get anaesthetised to its horror. But I understood, although back then I could never have put it into words, that Simpkins was making a case for the unexpected consequences of being there. The subjects had not just volunteered their bodies for dissection; they were brokering something in us, too – an appreciation of love and sacrifice; pathos rather than pathology. That was Flint's gift to us and Haselberry's gift to

Simpkins; they reminded all who beheld them of our humanity and mortality. That explained Charlie's tears, even before the old anatomist's intervention. I knew that Charlie must have been as moved as I was by his tale, but I couldn't work out how to introduce it into our conversation. It led to an awkward moment when I raised the subject of platonic love. Charlie just hmmed disinterestedly. Didn't she have a view, I wondered.

'That's the thing about language, isn't it?' she answered, 'funny how it can desert you when you need it most.'

It was my cue to shut up. We recovered our bonhomie quite speedily, though. But when she served out the meal I couldn't eat it. I felt peculiar suddenly, and feared I'd throw up. I had to lie down, I told her. There was no living room in her flat; just a shared kitchen. Charlie found a duvet, doubled it up and fashioned a space on the floor in her bedroom. She turned her back as I, with her insistence that I should be comfortable, took off my trousers and socks, and then laid down, folding the duvet around me. She drew the curtains; it was still only early evening and not yet dark, and placed a bowl beside me – 'just in case'. Charlie left on a lamp beside her bed but turned off the overhead light before quietly leaving the room. Within a little while I drifted off to the sound of her pottering around the kitchen.

I woke up a couple of hours later. Charlie must have crept back into her bedroom and into her bed; a book lay fallen on the floor beside her.

'You awake?' I whispered.

She didn't stir at first but then she pushed back the covers with her feet and stood up, needing the bathroom, I suppose. I half-closed my eyes but could see her pondering whether to put on a bathrobe; she couldn't be bothered. More than her nudity, I was impressed and surprised by how she stepped around me, moving easily and unselfconsciously as if she were fully clothed. I was ruminating on the night's unexpected turn of events when Charlie returned; she looked down defiantly at me, it seemed, until I opened my eyes. At which point she jumped back into her bed, knocking off the light.

'Don't ask.'

'Ask what?'

Charlie didn't answer. She was alone with her thoughts, and pretty soon, I was, too.

For a long while the silence lay heavily – like an uninvited guest who would not depart – between us.

'Did you ever have a time when you were a kid,' she asked eventually, 'when you thought you were invincible?' She didn't really leave space for me to answer, but expanded on the question, now asking me if I'd ever given any thought to how I might die. When I didn't immediately answer, she went back a few stages and questions, as we'd been taught at The London, to tease out a family, social and medical history from a reluctant patient. And finally she asked again, 'And what do your people die from?'

Charlie pushed further, repeating the question until I told her that most of my relatives who had died in recent years had not done so naturally.

'Really?'

I had her attention now. It was the truth. Members of our family did not succumb to cancer, heart or renal failure like 'reasonable' people. The most common form of death was murder. They died having been knifed by their own brother over an argument over washing up, or after drinking from a cocktail spiked with tiny bits of glass ground down by a vengeful lover. At least one had been shot by her husband in a dispute over an affair.

'When I go,' Charlie whispered, 'I'd like it to be sudden.' She fought back tears, and attempting to sound brighter continued, 'And what about your body? Would you leave that to science?'

I paused, scrambled up onto my knees and leaned over to kiss her. 'Please don't,' she said, and rolled onto her side away from me.

'What was that all about? Death and dying? What are you really saying?'

Charlie pulled her bed covers more tightly around her.

'Why did you hold my hand outside the dissection room if . . . ?' The words came out sharper than I intended.

'If? That's a bit of a leap, don't you think?' said Charlie. Her words jabbed and stung. She questioned whether I was really ill or whether it was just some ruse to gain her sympathy and to enable me to stay the night. She wanted to know if I made a habit of wanting to climb into bed with everyone whose hand I held. I said that we didn't have to do anything. 'I promise.'

'Very chivalrous of you, Mr Grant.'

'I'm serious.'

'Let's just keep it simple,' she said, throwing a pillow forcefully at me, 'and lessen the odds of you breaking your pledge.'

I bolted up and started hurriedly putting on my clothes.

'Now what?' She implored me to stay, half-heartedly I felt, whispering that I didn't have to go. And when I persisted, Charlie snapped, ordering me out, shouting that she couldn't bear my suffocating self-pity.

'What do you want from me?' she asked.

'What do you want from me?' I said coldly. 'A black trophy, an ornament? Add to your bona fides? Charlie? Yeah she's right on, she's cool. Only hangs out with black guys . . .' I stopped. I had gone too far.

'Just leave,' cried Charlie.

In the renewed silence, I could hear her quietly sobbing. But self-righteous fury drove me out of the room, out of her flat and out of her fucking life.

LESSON 4: Insert a finger between the costal cartilages and the pleura and separate the pleura from the inner surface of the ribs. With a saw cut through the manubrium, as high as possible, without damaging the clavicles.

I couldn't face going home. To resist turning on my heels and crawling back apologetically to Charlie's flat, I forced myself to head towards the college – which wouldn't close for another thirty minutes – and then straight up the stairs to the dissection room.

Trying to free the skin around Mr Flint's navel, I held its edge with tweezers and worked the blunt end of the scalpel just as Simpkins had shown us. But suddenly my arm snapped back of its own volition. I still held the tweezers but now there was a piece of flesh the size of a postage stamp trapped in its jaws. I'd pulled so hard that part of Flint's skin had sheared off. I looked over to the cadaver, half expecting Flint to cry out in pain. 'Now look what you've gone and done,' I imagined him saying. 'Silly sod.'

Whilst I was pondering my next move, the doors swung open and for a ridiculous moment I suspected Charlie might walk in. Instead a hand peeked through, felt for the light switches and began flicking them off. I cried out that I was still in the room. Mr Simpkins pushed on through the door, flicked the lights back on and shuffled over more slowly than before. He looked pitifully tired. I felt that if he'd had the energy to get up onto one of the tables and lay down, when I returned in the morning he'd have a label on his wrist and students would be working on his cadaver.

'Still here? Well, best you finish up and hurry along now. Mr Flint isn't going anywhere. He'll still be here in the morning.'

I reached for the green pouch and began slotting in the tools. When he asked me what I was doing there so late at night, anyway, I answered that I was a slow learner and was rerunning the day. He looked skeptical, but distracted. I asked him what he was doing so late in the dissection room.

'Touché,' he said and then went on to explain that sometimes he came by last thing just to say goodnight to the cadavers.

I noticed now, as he spoke, shuffling between the dissection tables, how he adjusted the sheets covering the cadavers, as if tucking in a half-asleep child.

I wanted to know how Simpkins could have spent more than half his lifetime, continuing to work here among the dead? How could he have empathy for them when he was cutting off their heads and sawing open their chests? How could he feel tender towards them?

'You bury the dead . . .'

'Yeah but you don't; they're still here.'

'They will be buried, what remains of them, at the end. You bury the dead, and take care of the living. It's as simple as that, isn't it? You dissect so you can take care of the living. That's what the people on these slabs wanted. That's why they bequeathed their bodies to us.'

I told Simpkins that I wouldn't do it, donate my body, not knowing what I knew now, seeing all the destruction.

'Are you all right?' he asked. 'You look out of sorts.'

I hesitated before answering that I'd tell him if he could be bothered to hear.

'Oh I can be bothered,' he said.

I explained that I'd been reflecting as usual, much to my

own annoyance, on the meaning of the day. Some days had more meaning, didn't they? This was one of them.

'One of those days?'

'Yes, and I've been thinking about what you said earlier, everything you said in fact.'

'Oh dear,' he chuckled.

I confessed that I'd been enchanted by his tale of meeting his wife, and, whilst he smiled graciously, I took a chance and confided that I'd begun to think of Mr Flint as a shadchan. I asked him what he thought about Charlie, and when he knew he would marry his wife?

Simpkins looked perplexed; he said he couldn't say. 'It's been a long day,' he answered.

The old anatomist encouraged me to gather my things. 'Medical school is a marathon run as a sprint,' he said. 'Need to keep your batteries charged.'

I played around with the slots in the dissection kit, reordering the tools in the pouch more than once, until Simpkins asked me if there was something else troubling me.

'Honestly?'

'Nothing better than . . .'

'Well there is one thing. The thing that most tires me, if you really want to know . . .'

'I do.'

'The thing that most tires me is being black. Well not exactly being black, but being thought of as black.'

'Aren't you black?' asked Simpkins.

'Yes, of course. I'm just tired of being thought of as black.'

Simpkins reflected on my words. I had been hesitant to speak to him, but perhaps that nervousness was unfounded. It was a relief to be able to surrender to someone wiser than myself. 'Sounds like an existential question.'

'Exactly. Exactly!'

'Yes, well,' Simpkins smiled: 'Not much we can do about that.'

Finally, I helped old Simpkins turn off the lights. I wanted to ask him more about his wife, but I guessed that she was dead. I guessed also that not a day passed without him calling her name or remembering their courtship in the dissection room and the first time he had held her hand. What a thrill it was to hold, however briefly, the unthinking hand that had once held yours.

Uncle Castus

Play fool fi ketch wise

Simpkins was never going to be the kind of man you could sit down with over a pint and work out, as a young and naive adult, how to live the kind of commendable life I imagined he'd had. That role was usually reserved for Uncle Castus who acted, when solicited, as a mentor; he was a ribald philosopher, who I saw as a version of Falstaff to my Prince Hal – more so when, at about the age of thirty, I realised that my Uncle Castus would have liked to have been me. He always said otherwise, but it was true. He teased me, claiming that I wasn't really black; that at best I was an 'alternate black'. What self-respecting black man, he wondered, would move to Brighton, ride a bike, prefer lentils to chicken, allow his children to call him by his first name, read feminist literature, give up the chance to become a doctor?

At the end of the first year Charlie transferred to medical school in Glasgow and I never saw her again. She had provided ballast in my wavering commitment to medicine, and in her absence, I was all at sea at the London Hospital. Each month, I'd an audience with the dean where I described my super-abundance of unhappiness. I'd fallen into the habit of going AWOL from time to time. The dean's eyebrows were perman-ently raised in bemusement, but they belied his patience. After each lapse he would encourage me to give it another try, to stick and stay. The last time I went AWOL though, on my return, I found the old dean had been replaced by an unsmiling younger man who thought his predecessor had been too lenient and that my attitude made a mockery of the noble profession. I agreed, and he was only too happy to accept, that I would resign from the college, to put the farce of my non-attendance to an end, and leave medicine forever.

Even years later, Uncle Castus never missed an opportunity to remind me of the folly of leaving, that I was a damn fool. 'You know how many black man would want what you have? Medicine, man! Medicine! You think I woulda walk away? You mad!' It was proof, as far as Castus was concerned that I could only do all the things of which he disapproved because of him. He told me, 'Somebody has to stand up and do the black thing.' And, warming to his theme, he continued with a phrase he'd often used before, 'I'm black so you can do all of those white things. I'm black so you don't have to be. It's a full-time occupation.' While instinctively and aesthetically I rejected Castus's premise, I sometimes wondered about it. Had the passage of time made it easier to 'code switch' and 'pass' as non-black? Perhaps. Castus and his generation, who arrived in the UK in the 1950s and 60s, were constantly made aware of their colour.

'Yes! We had more skin in the game,' agreed Castus, taking off his glasses to ensure that I understood the gravity of what he was about to say. 'This is some serious shit. Back then a black person was something. What is he now? Nothing special. Just like everyone else, whining about nothing.'

Back in the fabled cinnamon-scented past, Castus and his spars took setbacks and insults on the chin. Now they rolled their eyes at 'dis younger generation' and their 'whinging' about microaggressions at the hands of the white man. When I first received the invitation to join the BBC, Castus was not enthused. 'So you gwan to the dark side?' he mused. 'What kind of real black gwan work for the man? But then you is not really black, is you? What's your game? You gwan Mau Mau them or you gwan bend over blackwards, try fool them?'

I suggested to Castus that perhaps he was a little jealous. My uncle was certainly bright; his nickname in the family was 'two brains'. Ethlyn, his sister, used to coo: 'That bwoi have more diploma than John ever dream,' when recalling how her baby brother outsmarted his siblings as he grew up. Arriving in Britain, aged thirteen, though, the promise of Castus's youth, expressed in Jamaica, had not been fulfilled. He was never integrated into the British school system; his piece-meal education eked out during his lonely teenage years and early stop–start adulthood was marked by a series of high-minded specialist correspondence courses (unfathomable to Ethlyn and the Adamses). Somewhere in the late 1970s, Castus seemed to have dropped off our radar, and then more than a decade later, he'd turned up. One day, passing a dreary-looking off-licence beside St Clement's psychiatric hospital in Mile End, I caught sight of him behind the counter. Shocked, I lingered outside and out of sight for a long time, before I could steel myself to enter. Castus, bewilderingly, was the manager. When I walked in, he hardly looked up, in that cool laconic manner I'd come to associate with Jamaicans. If he was surprised to see me, he didn't let it show 'What'll it be?' He asked. 'Wine. I bet you drink wine. Chardonnay. I bet you drink spritzers.'

I did not, could not answer. Nor could I ask the real question he must have suspected I was bound to want an answer to: what had happened to you, to all that promise? Uncle Castus would have resented any sign of pity. That was all history, and, as he often asserted, 'There's no pity in history!' My eyes fell on the counter. A sacrificial altar? A chopping block? No. That counter was the coffin of his future. I was reacquainted with my uncle without the question being asked and we became fast friends once more.

Three years on, perhaps the philosopher wine merchant thought the BBC opportunity was wasted on me; and would have been more deserving for a righteous black man. But the job spec had my name all over it. After almost five years of toiling at The London Hospital, I'd left medicine, or, more accurately, medicine had left me, had shown me the door. I was doing odd jobs now and pushing thirty, and just the month before I'd started an adult education evening course in journalism. Kismet!

The advert in the *Guardian*'s jobs pages in the summer of 1989 looked promising. The BBC was looking to recruit some trainee radio producers. There was only one catch, but it was a good one: candidates needed to be 'of colour'. Well, those weren't the actual words in the advert, but they were implied. A simple hand-drawn, black-and-white illustration accompanied the advert. A black African man in an outfit made of kente cloth sat at a round table opposite a woman of South Asian origin, wearing a sari. In the middle of the table was a microphone, emitting lightning-like flashes of transmission to a globe of the world above the heads of the two presenters. The advert was clumsy, but seemed well intentioned. It was part of a recent recruitment drive, as reported in *The Times* 'to ensure the ethnic make-up of [the BBC's] workforce reflects the nation it serves'. I sent in an application to become one of the six trainees.

In truth, applying felt fraudulent. The Radio Journalist Trust would place successful applicants in departments of the BBC World Service. Growing up in Luton, I was only familiar with the BBC's two television channels and popular, if lame, Radio stations 1 and 2. I only became aware of the other cultural strands, middlebrow Radio 4 and elitist Radio 3, when I attended medical school; on Sunday mornings students tended to divide into two camps – those who took an ironic interest in Radio 4's *The Archers*, and a smaller tribe who sang along knowingly and loudly to 'Madam Butterfly' and other operatic warbles on Radio 3. But even then, the existence of the former Empire Service had escaped me. Prior to applying to join the Corporation, more than half a century after its launch, I'd never heard about it. King George V may have intended that the service would communicate with 'men and women, so cut off by the snow, the desert, or the sea, that only voices out of the air can reach them' but what about Luton? The World Service's reach had not extended to Farley Hill.

Now, I marvel at my ignorance, but back then I didn't seem to be alone. At the interview, it helped that I'd an ace up my sleeve: a letter of endorsement from the former assistant head of the BBC's radio drama department. By happenstance, I'd become a tennis-playing partner of Hallam Tennyson, the great-grandson of the poet, Alfred Lord Tennyson. I suppose as a twenty-something-year-old, I'd inadvertently flattered the soon-to-be seventy-year-old, formerly married but now openly gay man, through regularly answering his invitations to play at his north London tennis club. I hadn't outwardly stated my heterosexuality, thinking it vulgar and presumptuous to do so. 'Big mistake,' was Uncle Castus's verdict. 'Check your shoes, you're stepping in shit!' I explained to Castus that he, Castus, was unreconstructed; it was perfectly reasonable for a heterosexual to befriend a gay man. Castus replied that I was an idiot.

Even so, my friendship with Hallam had cooled a little when, after a knock-up on the courts, I'd accompanied him to his apartment to receive a copy of his autobiography. I'd offered previously to buy it at a bookshop but Hallam was adamant that I should have a signed copy. I hesitated but followed him falteringly into his bedroom where the memoir was to be found among hundreds of copies stacked from floor-to-ceiling in a bulging wardrobe. I remember making a mental note that publishing was obviously a fantasist's or fool's profession. Later, reading Hallam Tennyson's graphic descriptions of the male anatomy and the suffusion of bodily fluids through the text, illustrating and underpinning revelations of his unbridled promiscuity since coming out, unnerved me. I'd stopped answering Hallam's calls but he was generous and gracious enough to answer my call for a reference to attach to the BBC application.

If they'd closed their eyes the all-white middle-aged panel might have assumed that, aside from a tendency to say 'aks' instead of 'ask', I was really one of them. But blackness is not something you can put on and take off like a robe, and their eyes were wide open. Still, I could see and take advantage of that familiar, decent, liberal middle-class yearning to be confounded; for their expectations to be turned upside down. I pitched the story of myself as an 'educated' but still 'street' black man, and they ate it up. I was in!

'So you really *are* gwan do the Uncle Tom thing?' said Castus.

I didn't understand Castus's antipathy. This was low-hanging fruit, after all. I told my clever uncle that had he been in my position, he'd have picked the fruit and nyam it one time.

'Me?' Castus exploded. 'Babylon nah have no fruit.'

'You can't just steal Marley's words and parrot them as your own.'

'I come from before brother Bob, you hear. I come from time.'

Sometimes I felt that Castus and I were the same person. He was only fourteen years older than me and often it seemed that we were more brothers than uncle and nephew. I knew that, really, I was lucky; Castus was just as bright and talented (more so in his opinion) than me. But institutions like the BBC were not interested in finding men like him in the 1960s and 70s when he'd been in his prime.

Castus had one final word of warning about the BBC, and Britain in general, using the black man when it suited him. 'Remember Joe Bygraves!' Castus trotted out the familiar story (I'd heard a thousand times) of the perfidy of the English. When the Jamaican-born boxer was doing well and winning medals for Britain, he was *British*, but as soon as he was knocked to the floor in a final match, the English commentators had exclaimed, 'The Jamaican is down!' 'You can play fool fi ketch wise in the Bombaclaat Broadcasting Corporation,' Castus concluded. 'Jus' mek sure you don't catch some licks!'

I had worked for the BBC for fifteen years when my second letter of invitation arrived; it was not so welcome. There are some letters that should never be opened; either they're triggers that will set off chain reactions or they're bombs. The BBC insignia on the envelope was the first warning; I had a hunch about what lay inside. Now that the moment had arrived, I realised I should have seen it coming. The pleasure of the big reveal could only be deferred for one coffee. How can you open a letter yet hide the contents from yourself?

I took a knife and sliced open the envelope. 'Dear Colin,' the letter began, 'I am inviting you to a disciplinary hearing . . .'

Bomb it was, then. The immediate effect was both unusual and familiar. Students will recognise that moment of trepidation in the exam hall when they turn over the exam paper to read a question they cannot comprehend or begin to shape an answer for; they read the question again, trying somehow to rearrange the words to make it sensible. I gobbled up the BBC letter, attempting to redraft each sentence that flashed by. The wall of the living room started to crumble, a great fissure opened up in the floor, the house collapsed, and I was left naked.

I had signed for the recorded-delivery letter, like an unwitting spouse served with divorce papers. The letter was more than a threat of separation; the enclosed invitation was to answer questions raised into serious allegations from a manager that I had behaved aggressively towards her. The use of the word 'inviting' seemed ironic, for this was not an invitation I could refuse.

My name and aggression had never once formed part of the same sentence. The man described in the letter was an impostor. I wasn't a gold-toothed, skanking street hustler. I'd been an altar boy for seven years, head boy at junior and senior school and had toiled away as a student at The London and at the BBC for more years than I cared to remember. I didn't fit the lazy profile of an aggressive black youth, but perhaps this was actually the way I had been perceived from the very beginning of my career.

My initial invitation to join the Corporation had marked a milestone: it made up somewhat for my failure to complete the course at medical school. There were a few caveats. Although venerating the BBC, my family understood that not only was the organisation a 'white space', but it employed the kind of people who thought it acceptable to entertain the nation on Saturday nights with *The Black and White Minstrel Show*, featuring white men with shoe-polished black faces and bowler hats dancing with long-legged white women. It was doubtful, too, that the Auntie-knows-best educators of public taste had us in mind when they commissioned the 1970s sitcom *The Good Life*. Where even was Surbiton? And was there much difference anyway between off-the-grid, home-knitting, pig-rearing Tom and Barbara, and their stiff, fusspot, permanently evening-gowned and dinner-jacketed neighbours, Margot and Jerry. Both were allegedly benign and peculiarly British.

At medical school I'd only ever met a handful of 'oddballs': women and men, mostly English, who revelled in their eccentricities. I never thought so at the time, but such eccentrics would have found their equivalents among my parents' West Indian peers: men such as Tidy Boots, who was forever fussy about his footwear. 'Characters' were thick on the ground in the World Service. The international broadcasting organisation's HQ at Bush House was home to: asylum seekers who'd smuggled themselves out of their repressive homelands; intellectuals whose genius did not extend to self-presentation; nerds who competed in how speedily they might recite the names of the entire shadow cabinet of St Kitts and Nevis; and a managing director, a charming yet shrewd aesthete, whose elegance evoked Fred Astaire. Scattered throughout the building, their numbers were greater in units such as Arts and Features and Science, where individualism and specialism were encouraged.

Our traineeship was focused on news and current affairs in departments where, although people might have been bullish, there was the overwhelming sense of being subsumed into a group identity, in the service of an ennobling idea bigger than any individual. As one of the chosen, passing through the portico of Bush House seemed a giddying privilege. Was the inscription above the entrance to the grand neo-classical building, 'To the Friendship of English-speaking Peoples', pompous?

No, it was welcoming. The building gave off a satisfied hum, as did the employees, including me.

For someone of my complexion in 1990s Britain, the trick for joining the BBC was to embark on one of two strategies, just as Uncle Castus had outlined: show that you were a present threat, but hint that your threat level would decline once you'd been co-opted into the institution and catapulted onto the greasy pole of promotion; or project that you constituted no threat from the start. I chose the latter route. It wasn't difficult; I'd taken the 'be liked' path, as directed by my parents, most of my life.

After two years of traineeship, I gravitated towards the newsroom, and joined the ranks of the freelance 'casuals'. Arranged in a semi-circle around the 'centre desk', where the editors and their top writers sat, were upwards to a hundred journalists, almost all of them men, a handful of women and not one black or brown face. The staff were habituated to it, but senior officials were not unaware of the strangeness of the impression it left on outsiders given a tour of the newsroom. Along with the five other trainees, I had been the beneficiary of the BBC's desire for change.

Throughout the traineeship, we'd been conscious to not strut around like prized peacocks, but we were nonetheless conspicuous, on permanent display, prized by management. No doubt we were resented by some for what they imagined to be our speedy trajectory through the Corporation whilst they – older, more talented and more deserving but without the benefit of pigment – toiled away on the 'regional desks' with the likelihood of promotion to the 'centre desk' being glacial.

Stepping into the building, I was always struck by its Tardis-like quality. It encapsulated an era of British imperialism, which, outside of Bush House, had mostly been laid to rest. No doubt it surfaced in other boardrooms and institutions that I wasn't privy to. At the World Service, the lingering grandeur of the country's imperial past was reflected in the marble floors and Corinthian columns of Bush House, a symbol of the best of world civilisation, transcending national borders and hovering somewhere above the globe, broadcasting without prejudice or favour.

The newsroom produced news summaries and bulletins in English. It was the nerve centre of the building, and the forty Language Services and Sections took their cue from it. They could tailor their output according to regional interests but the headline news stories were always prescribed, determined by the newsroom. The centre was holding, for now. The imperial hangover was also reflected in the composition of the person-nel in the language sections: the staff were invariably from the region targeted in their broadcasts but the heads of the sections were mostly white, British men, from the Home Counties. Some had the manner of viceroys, dispatched to outposts of civilisation, and some were more like missionary vicars.

The newsroom seemed to be populated by these viceroys and vicars straight out of central casting. I preferred the vicars who were at least nice even when they were being patronising. The first time I wrote a news story for a bulletin, the vicar–editor assigned to oversee my work came to my desk, and, over my shoulder, read the story on the terminal. When he finished reading he beamed and cooed, 'This is actually quite good!'

Clearly, the smartest, and possibly safest, way to proceed with a career in the BBC was to 'play fool fi ketch wise', to skin your teet' in a Hollywood cheesecake smile, to be a perfect pic-ture of discretion, always; and no answering back. Castus had come round to my way of thinking – kind of.

'Whenever an editor looks over your copy and says incredulously, "You know this is actually quite well written",' Castus advised, 'resist the temptation to finish his sentence with "for a black man".'

The World Service saw itself as the world's broadcaster. In the glorious past, reports may have begun with the station identification: 'This is London . . .' followed reassuringly by 'Lilliburlero', but now it promoted the fiction that somehow it was untethered from any landmass and was broadcasting from the stratosphere. The international broadcaster carried no brief for any country; it was neutral, and in a news bulletin, the King of Swaziland would be accorded the same respect as the King of Spain. I was surprised, then, when writing a news story about Elizabeth II, Queen of the United Kingdom that I was upbraided by an irate vicar: 'It's just the Queen; everyone knows who the Queen is!'

I did not challenge him and I willingly signed up for the code, which David Caute identified in his 1986 novel *News from Nowhere*. 'Do they have censors in the BBC ?' one of the characters asks. 'No,' comes the sad reply, 'they make you do it yourself.'

If anyone had asked me my specialisation at this time (they didn't), I'd have answered that I specialised in the art of biting my tongue. This even extended to a deadpan face when, over a pint in the World Service bar after a newsroom shift, an editor informed the assembled colleagues holding onto his every word: 'Of course, Bob Marley's career only took off when he covered Eric Clapton's "I Shot the Sheriff".'

A few weeks later, after I'd failed to correct this inversion of the truth, another Jamaican story was blasted over the tannoy in the newsroom. It was 1992 and news wires around the world screamed with the headlines that Jamaica had gained her first black prime minister. The thrilling news of P. J. Patterson's elevation marked a great reversal of fortunes for black people in Jamaica. During the height of the Atlantic Slave Trade, 600,000 Africans were abducted and brought to this Caribbean island, more than were shipped to North America. Now, hundreds of years later one of their descendants had become the most important person on the island for the first time. There was only one small problem with that romantic narrative: it wasn't true.

I was on a trial shift on the centre desk, much to the amazement of some seasoned figures in the newsroom who'd not yet been offered such a prize. When the news about Patterson came through, I was alarmed to see that the BBC was considering broadcasting this terrible mistake and, worse still, I was being asked to write it up. I stood and went to the editor's desk. 'P. J. Patterson is not the first black prime minister of Jamaica,' I whispered. He asked me to speak up, so I exclaimed, 'P. J. Patterson is not the first black prime minister of Jamaica. He just succeeded Michael Manley who was elected prime minister twenty years ago.'

'But Manley wasn't black,' said the editor.

'What?' I was perplexed. 'He was. He was!'

The editor leaned over to the news agency desk, to the reams of copy coming off the machines. Reuters, Associated Press, every single agency was reporting the same breaking news about P. J. Patterson's elevation.

'I can't write that,' I said. 'I just can't.'

The editor sighed, and looked at the clock. There were only a few minutes before the next world news bulletin. He held out his hand, pointing to the news copy about Patterson on my desk. I gave it to him and he handed the copy to Clarke, one of the fastest and most-revered journalists.

Nothing, especially not the intervention of a junior writer who just graduated from a traineeship, was going to stop this juggernaut of news. Clarke dashed off the story and rushed to the newsreader's booth just in time, before the pips. I seem to remember applause coming from others on the centre desk.

It was time for a break. The editor gathered his things and headed out towards the lifts, out of the newsroom. I traipsed after him, still protesting. 'But Michael Manley is black. He's mixed race; he's not white.'

'Are you following me?' He asked. 'Really?'

I was aware that I'd refused an *instruction* to write up a news story and sought urgently to explain why. Now that the tense moment had passed, I was beginning to realise its dangerous implications for my future; I wanted to also reassure him that the breach of protocol – a rush of blood to the head – was a one-off. The editor liked me, he said, and he wouldn't take the matter further, but warned me that I mustn't fuck up again. I found myself, to my later dismay, apologising. A lift had come and gone. We were still waiting for the next one, when Clarke breezed through the newsroom doors and came to stand behind us. 'That was a close shave,' he said.

There was kudos attached to a position on the centre desk. But let's not forget, any job amongst the top cats of the newsroom was pretty damn cool, and when, not long afterwards, I was promoted to chief sub-editor, my sister, Shirley, rang excitedly to tell me: 'You gone clear!' She meant that I'd made it; I couldn't be touched now.

Shirley was right. Daily, there were moments to swell the head of a young black man who, having dropped out of medical school, seemed – miraculously – to have landed on his feet. Other black people in the building appeared to take vicarious pleasure in my elevation. I exchanged the black nod with the uniformed commissionaires at reception, especially Caleb, who always greeted me with, 'Good morning, sir, welcome back.' The BBC was a great validator. Bush House was both a citadel and a place of safety, even if it wasn't always safe outside.

The newsroom night shift, reviewing and writing up the featured stories from the early morning newspapers, was always a favourite of mine. But leaving for home at 4 a.m. there was always a part of London, a row of streets heading east between Fleet Street and the Thames, where the chances were I'd be stopped by the police on my way to Wapping. Lately, I'd taken to driving north away from my Wapping flat and then arching back towards it via Shoreditch, circumnavigating the patrolling policemen. It added another ten minutes onto the journey but it was worth it; to avoid the aggravation. On the last night shift of the month, though, I thought to chance my luck and take the most direct route home via the Embankment.

I'd lost count of the number of times I'd been stopped driving by the equivalent of Constable Savage from a *Not the Nine O'Clock News* sketch who arrests the same man hundreds of times for offences which included being in possession of 'thick lips and curly hair'.

Stop and search was promoted as an effort to drive down crime; and there were plenty of black people of Bageye's generation who argued that some of the bad-bwois, the muggers and burglars, had brought it on themselves; and that if the rest of the yout' were now subject to 'sufferation' then so be it. 'You're being watched,' Bageye had reminded us in our own youth, 'to see which way you turn.'

Of course, my father was a man who 'love to tek chance', and was adept at distracting and amusing whichever officer stopped his car with an immediate promotion to detective inspector.

I turned onto the side street leading to the Embankment, and saw a pair of policemen: a bearded elder and a younger one, straight out of the Met's Hendon training school, I imagined. I told myself not to be so foolish as to stop and reverse. I was conscious that I was driving a Ford Capri with a lime-green body and chocolate-brown vinyl roof that might attract their attention.

They waved me down. I pulled over and stepped out of the car. Six feet and rising. Suspect? And yet there was a tiny hesitation. Something didn't seem right. My wire-rimmed John Lennon glasses, perhaps? And then there was the voice. My accent – more 'speaking clock' than black South London – didn't quite fit. I prepared myself for the faux respect, and was not disappointed. The younger policeman, a black man, was an unwelcome complication. There used to be a handbook given out to recruits at the Met's Hendon Training Centre on how to interpret black men – in their stance, the way they hold themselves, the sounds they make, and the language they use. But you can't legislate for the arrogance of a black policeman who believes his colour gives him an interpretative advantage when dealing with his kith and kin.

At some level, I felt sorry for him and settled on at least affecting a conciliatory tone.

'Morning officer, is there a problem?'

His gaze seemed to be directed to a point to the right of my ear: 'You do know there are cobwebs on your bumper?'

'Cobwebs on my bumper?' I repeated back the words slowly.

'Yes, cobwebs on your bumper.'

'On my bumper?'

'Yes.'

I could hear the sound of my father whispering in my ear.

'Detective Inspector, are you really stopping me because there are cobwebs on my bumper?'

The policeman bristled. 'There's no need to get snarky, is there, mate.'

'Who are you calling mate?'

'Who are you calling Detective Inspector?'

'OK, Constable, so you're stopping me because there are cobwebs on my bumper?'

'Yes, where's this car been parked?'

By now a police van had pulled up alongside us. The elder policeman demanded my driving licence and walked over with it to the van. There was some exchange between him and the officers inside and when he returned he said pointedly: 'This car is registered in Luton. Did you lose your way?'

It would be a while before I could calm myself enough to answer, and was surprised to hear myself barking at the policeman that cobwebs were not an indication of fucking criminality and that it should not matter where the car was fucking registered; that I was free to drive where I bloody well chose to. I don't recall now why the policemen didn't arrest me and how I eventually got back to Wapping. The next day, despite the welcome from Caleb, when I walked back into the World Service, I did not feel so special. Speaking later with Castus, he wondered what I could have expected, trying to play my father's trick.

'Bageye would have come across as a little, humble working-class West Indian,' said Castus. '"Detective Inspector?" You saying that, you come across as a sneering, middle-class twat.'

Here then, was the dilemma of being black, even if your uncle had assured you that you didn't have to be. You were invisible, rarely found in white spaces and professions not historically associated with people of pigment. But you were also in danger of being hyper-visible, especially to policemen on the street, when all you wanted to do was to go about your business unmolested.

At the World Service, you could feel sullied beyond its gates, but cleansed when you stepped back inside. After working in the newsroom, I became a radio producer, making arts, science and current affairs magazine programmes and documentaries. I made good friends, no matter their colour; I found my people, as Ethlyn had advised. Working for Auntie was still fun, a privilege and an education.

Without the World Service, I'd never have borrowed a pair of swimming trunks from the founder of Island Records, Chris Blackwell, whilst I awaited our interview and swam at Jamaica's Golden Eye; or returned to my old medical school in East London to reconnect with Simpkins, the elderly, tender anatomist in making a documentary on the art of dissection; or sat on the verandah with Derek Walcott in St Lucia, listening to him recite poems in the wine-dark night; or watched from the window of Philip Glass's townhouse as he bounded down a street in lower Manhattan so as not to be late to meet me; or been given the chance to sharpen my writing when conjuring the life and death of Federico García Lorca; or interviewed and been enveloped by the warmth and wisdom of Toni Morrison.

Without the World Service, I'd never have known about my predecessors from the Caribbean, producers and presenters in the 1940s and 50s; figures such as Una Marson, Learie Constantine and George Lamming, who had campaigned for radio coverage from and to the West Indies, as well as the inclusion of 'black Englishmen' in the BBC Home Service radio broadcasts, for a future, imagined me.

Without the World Service, it's unlikely I'd have considered the importance of patronage as exhibited in the glorious days of 'Caribbean Voices', a literary programme, once edited by V.S. Naipaul, designed for audiences in the West Indies, and which only came to a close, announced the BBC, when it was clear that, 'the children had outgrown the patronage of the parent'.

Without the World Service, I wouldn't have been able to give a chance to inexperienced freelance reporters, with no industry contacts and backgrounds similar to mine, who'd previously had no luck trying to convince other producers of their merits. And but for the World Service, I'd never have had a homecoming of sorts when I travelled to Africa for the first time, to Burkina Faso, 'the land of incorruptible people'.

In a sense that's how I saw the BBC: a space occupied by incorruptible people. After my first decade in the Corporation, I was eventually lulled into thinking that no one paid any attention to my colour; I was not a black producer but simply Colin. I'd even begun to think of myself as a permanent and known fixture in the Corporation, but one Christmas that myth was punctured.

As I ambled towards a radio workshop at the top of the building, I passed a fellow producer (known to me by sight). He stopped and turned back to me and said: 'Are you looking for a computer?' My first thought was: crikey, I know there's hot-desking but has it come to hot-computing? I didn't really know what he meant and mumbled that no, I was on my way to a workshop. I noticed a few things we had in common: he was probably about my age; we both wore neatly pressed long-sleeved shirts (mine was plain, his pin-striped); and both had soft southern voices – his only slightly more posh than mine.

A few minutes later, I was still puzzling over the comment

'Are you looking for a computer?' when, peering through the workshop window into the office, I saw the producer – now at his desk – and an engineer from the IT department attending him; and a hot flush of recognition washed over me, that my fellow producer had mistaken me for a technician from computer support. In a sense the producer's myopia, if not forgivable, was understandable. The hierarchy of the BBC reflected the population: high-end positions – producers, editors and managers – tended to be held by white people; black staff were overrepresented in the canteen, as commissionaires and IT/computer support. Looking over the open-plan room now I saw that not one of the twenty or so staff in the producer's department was black.

There *were* black and brown producers in the Language Services and Sections – Caribbean, Hausa, Hindi and Urdu, and many more. But I was among only a handful of producers of colour in the English Language Service. The white producer who failed to recognise me was part of the paternalistic old boys' club who ran things; there was even a club called the Bushmen. I didn't join. There came a time, though, when the World Service began to change, when managers, untainted by experience, were parachuted in with more 'modern' methodologies and who used words like 'metric'. Out went the polite, if patronising patrician types and in came thin-skinned, sharp elbowed contrarians. More women managers were brought into this new system – a seemingly enlightened and welcome development – but theirs was often an administrative role rather than creative; they'd been brought in to count the beans. Too late did producers like me wake up to the realisation that we were in the midst of a culture war within Bush House. The World Service began to more closely resemble the world outside.

*

Halfway into my career, I was tasked with overseeing a presenter's interview with the Jamaican-born opera singer, Sir Willard White. Towards the end of the interview, she asked Sir Willard about how the performance landscape had changed for black stage actors: 'Ten years ago, Sir Willard, there were hardly any black actors on the British stage; now we have a black Henry IV at the RSC, a black Sky Masterson in *Guys and Dolls* at the National Theatre. Things have improved, haven't they?' Willard White glared at her before answering: 'You tell me! I wasn't in the room when they decided who they were going to let through. You white people control things, so you tell me!'

Radio gold! The presenter and I celebrated in the bar afterwards, as we'd gotten some heat; we'd recorded a raw exchange that would bring a rare bit of passion and truth to our sanitised airwaves. The interview, recorded on quarter-inch studio magnetic tape, was subsequently dispatched to 'continuity', a room where the tapes were lined up on reel-to-reel machines, ready for transmission at the weekend. A day later, I received a phone call from a colleague. In a strained voice and with a heavy heart, he told me that the unit manager had heard about the exchange, and had ordered a razor blade to be taken to the tape recording, and the offending passage of tape dumped in a bin – apparently to spare the presenter's 'blushes'.

What was I to do about this soft censorship? Take the path of righteous dissent and call out editorial cowardice? Or plump for the wisdom of silence, the kind once characterised by Seamus Heaney as 'the government of the tongue'? On returning to work, I managed just to hold my tongue.

Prior to the arrival of the new manager, we'd worked in small groups of four or five, almost hermetically sealed in book-lined offices, in a discrete and civilised environment. The new manager came in with fresh ideas to knock down internal walls to create a huge, open-plan space. Privately, my colleagues were outraged, but at a meeting to discuss the plans, nobody demurred. When it was my turn to speak, I said I didn't like open-plan offices because it made me think of plantation life, with the overseer in the big house looking out over the slaves toiling in the cotton fields. Everybody, apart from the manager, laughed.

After the meeting the manager chased after me, cornered and then corralled me into a small workshop. When the door was closed, there was no room even to turn around. We were only inches apart. I could feel her warm breath on my face as she struggled to contain her rage.

'How dare you accuse me of wanting to be a slave owner!'

Recounting the episode to my uncle later that evening, he chastised me for being so foolish. What if, my uncle wanted to know, the manager later claimed that, in that tiny workshop, I'd touched her?

'Don't be daft. This is the BBC, not—'

'Not what?' Uncle Castus interrupted. 'Not an Antebellum plantation?'

A week later, I received the invitation to the disciplinary hearing. The complaint was that I exhibited 'a pattern of behaviour which might be regarded as aggressive [and] can be perceived as hostile, in terms of your tone of voice or body language'. The hearing's process and protocols were rather quaint. A booklet, accompanying the letter, outlined what to expect now that I'd been identified as a suspect.

Within minutes of receiving the invitation, I phoned and left a message for the sender, a senior manager (the manager's manager, – let's call him 'The Man') who, I'd later discover, would act on her behalf as the plaintiff; he'd also volunteer himself to be the chief prosecutor and, for good measure, the judge as well. But all that was in the future; for now, we were still within the realm of possibly resolving the situation locally. The Man rang me back later that afternoon at my desk. I took a deep breath, assembled my thoughts and whispered down the line that there must have been a terrible mistake. I was friendly and unaggressive, as my colleagues would attest.

The Man let me speak on and on, without interruption. Finally, I suggested to him that perhaps we could go for a drink in the bar and sort it out over a pint. There was a pause before he answered: 'No, I don't think that's right. I wouldn't want you to say anything to compromise your case.' I detected glee in his voice.

Naturally that evening, I asked for Castus's advice: 'What does it mean?'

'What does it mean? You don't know?' Castus just about stifled a laugh.

'No, that's why I'm asking.'

'It means you're fucked!'

'Would you care to clarify?'

'Let's just say, the brother doesn't want to sit around taking tea with you with a napkin in his lap and a china plate of cucumber sandwiches with the crust cut off, fool,' said Castus. 'No, he wants to take you round the corner in the dead of night and introduce you to the finer points of a baseball bat.'

'Don't hold back,' I said to my uncle, 'give it to me straight.'

Castus needed little encouragement. 'He hates you, and for good reason. For centuries he's used you as the middle-man, to keep the nasty naygars at bay. But push come to shove my friend, the minute you show you are more inclined towards Geronimo than Sitting Bull you are well and truly fucked. If I was you I'd, I dunno, maybe make up some bullshit, plead stress, apologise profusely.'

'But I haven't done anything wrong,' I said.

'Oh, brother!'

Castus's words were no less unsettling for being absurd. I told him that I wasn't going to be intimidated into making stuff up and genuflecting.

'Your funeral,' said Castus. 'Dem sure to scalp you. When are you going to wake up to the fact that though you think you're white, you're not, not like them?'

'C'mon. Don't give me that!'

For the first stage of the hearing, The Man appointed a stony-faced 'impartial' investigator with experience in 'matters of race relations'.

'What three words best describe you?' asked the investigator.

I didn't care for the question – introduced, she said, as an opening gambit, 'Just to get things started.'

'Tall and black,' I answered, straining and failing to curb a sarcastic tongue.

'And?' She persisted. 'A third word?'

'I'm not playing this game.'

'Tall, yes. Black, yes.' She spoke as a teacher might when encouraging a child with a limited vocabulary. 'And?'

'Just tall and black.'

'And aggressive? Would that be a fair description: "aggressive"?'

I didn't respond.

She tried again. 'Are you surprised to hear you've been described as aggressive?'

'No.'

The investigator sat forward. 'No? You're not surprised?'

204

'No.'

'She says she felt you were being aggressive towards her.'

'I wasn't.'

'Yes, but she felt you were. If she genuinely felt you to be aggressive, then you were, weren't you?'

I struggled with the investigator's logic, with her knight's-move thinking. But more than being confused by it, I resented it. And I was suddenly aware, in a way that I hadn't been before, that the woman from HR who sat beside the investigator was making notes. Her pen, poised above the paper, now paused.

'Take your time,' said the investigator. 'Think carefully.'

I did think, and the more I did so, the more discursive I became. I did myself no favours by objecting to the remit of the hearing and the use of the word 'aggressive' as a suitable descriptor for me. For too long, I argued, that word had been levelled at all black people. It was part of the code to keep us in our place.

'If I had been tall, white and Oxbridge-educated, you'd say I was assertive. I'll accept "assertive". But "aggressive"? No.'

My inquisitor nodded. 'So you are accusing your manager of being racist, is that right?' As well as being investigated for my aggression, she now spelled out that they'd also be considering my allegation of racism.

'But I haven't made any such allegation,' I answered.

'This is a serious matter,' said the investigator. 'We take such accusations very seriously. It could have serious consequences for the person in question.'

'But I haven't made any accusations.'

'So you're withdrawing your complaint?'

'There was no complaint.'

The investigator seemed to brighten. 'Yes, right then, we'll consider it withdrawn,' she said, and directed the silent note-taker to strike my non-allegation from the records.

This would be the tone throughout the weeks and months of the hearing, which was already beginning to feel like a trial. As the trial progressed – every employee who'd worked with me in the past five years was asked their opinion of my character – other incidents of my alleged aggressive behaviour were put forward for consideration.

Sleep disappeared, to be replaced by a permanent state of anxiety. Each Friday afternoon I rang the HR person, hoping to hear that the investigation had been completed, but he said he couldn't enlighten me. I rang The Man and he referred me to the investigator. I rang the investigator and she directed me back to The Man. I wrote to The Man and told him that I'd given the investigator a list of three witnesses to the alleged incidence of aggression but she had not interviewed any of them. The Man wrote back to me with a curt and self-satisfying letter, asking me how I knew my witnesses had not been interviewed, and reminded me that the investigation was confidential. I stopped sleeping altogether.

I had been naïve. I had assumed that the difficulty of getting into the BBC was the main problem, but that once you were in, then you were safe. I hadn't stopped to consider that the BBC was still a microcosm of British society, and that there were people inside this liberal institution who would continue to view me, a black man, with suspicion. Somewhere along the line in my adult life I was bound to have had to answer this charge. You are a black man; eventually someone is going to label you 'aggressive'. When your accuser is a white woman, you will be doubly indicted. There is the actuality of the contemporary allegation itself to contend with, but also the historical one; for black men over centuries have been charged with menacing or interfering with white women. I should have seen it coming.

During the following week, it became clear that an old, familiar trope was being played out; the lustful and aggressive black man threatening the intimidated white woman, a fragrant damsel in distress, in danger of being molested, in need of a chivalric saviour.

The hearing rolled on and on interminably. I believed I was liked, but I was surprised by how guarded colleagues were with me now. Perhaps they saw a dead man walking and didn't know how to approach him or show sympathy. From the disciplinary booklet it was clear that managers would have actively discouraged my colleagues from doing anything that might 'compromise the investigation'. Everyone who'd worked with me in recent years was to be interviewed and asked whether they believed me to be aggressive. A few friends, Emma, Nick and Olive, were brave enough to demonstrate their continued faith in me, and offered counsel, but I was mostly disappointed by the rest. When I complained to my Uncle Castus about my feeling of abandonment, he answered simply: 'When the lights go on the cockroaches scatter.'

Over the months of interrogation, it became increasingly clear that I was not being scrutinised for my aggression; rather, I was on trial for not fitting in, for having duped them. I was not the pliant soul they had believed me to be when I had accepted the invitation to join the Corporation; I was not one of them. It was as if I were a Trojan Horse, let through the gates of Bush House into the sacred space of the institution. I'd only fully revealed myself once I was safely inside and was now bent on burning down the master's house. The managers had realised, too late, their mistake. The retrograde invitation to a disciplinary hearing was a manifestation of that.

Six months after the investigation began, I was summoned to The Man's office to hear the verdict. As I took a seat, he barely looked up. His eyes were fixed on a sheet of paper. He slowly read out the full details of the original and expanded terms of the inquiry. Finally, he lifted his head, took off his glasses and sighed: 'The charge against you is not proven.'

I'd survived. It was proposed that it would be better for everybody if I was moved to another department. I agreed. There was a sense of relief. I admitted to myself that I'd evaded The Man and his ilk for more years than most, whilst suspecting that this moment was always going to come. Even though I'd emerged with the verdict 'unproven', I hadn't triumphed, not really. Truthfully, I'd been humiliated and traduced; they and The Man had won – but at least there was no more harm to be done.

A month or so after the move, I decided to go back to my old department to collect my things to bring them over to my new department. I still had my key, and I went into my old office on the weekend; I didn't want to see any of the old colleagues who had scattered when the lights came on during my investigation. I took my time in the office, lingering over the space for the last time, where I'd mostly had happy experiences. I felt mournful now. I took a break from packing and read the Saturday *Guardian*. There was a sad feature about the temporary disappearance and delicate mental state of the footballer, Sol Campbell, and the precariousness of black people who rise in professions only, inevitably, to fall.

There were too many books and artefacts in the office to remove; in the end I only managed to half-fill the box and made a mental note to return the following weekend. On Monday morning, I received an animated phone call at home from a friend in my old office. 'You're in trouble, Colin,' she said. It transpired in the last few months some books had gone missing from the office and The Man had persuaded the department to install CCTV cameras. I had entered my old office, ignorant of the new surveillance, and had now been 'caught on camera' taking away a box that included books. I told my friend not to worry, it was laughable; it was all my own stuff.

She advised me to call The Man, anyway. I did so, reluctantly; I wasn't keen on ever hearing his voice again. But it was a funny coincidence – me clearing out my old desk and shelves on the first weekend when surveillance cameras were installed – and I fully, naïvely, expected him to laugh along with me. Before I was halfway through my explanation, though, The Man interrupted: 'I don't think it advisable that you say any more,' he said. 'I wouldn't want you to compromise yourself.'

The Man was a big cat; I was a small bird he had caught and trapped in his mouth. I was wounded, but he wasn't going to kill me straight away; he would play with me first.

Uncle Castus reminded me that 'history has a way of repeating itself first as tragedy, then as farce'. But the circumstances of the first disciplinary hearing had been farcical from the start. The farce of the second hearing unfolded as déjà vu, even down to the detail of The Man acting as the accuser, the prosecutor and judge. Awaiting the interrogation with The Man, who this time would question me himself, I was ushered into a room by myself to review the grainy footage from the CCTV cameras. Looking at the film was uncanny. I felt tender towards my ghostly apparition, the naïve innocent who sat in his old office reading the Saturday paper and half-heartedly packing a box of his things, with no inkling of the fierce storm that was heading his way, and would soon engulf him.

Thankfully, the hearing only ran on for a few weeks. In the final judgement, even though my theft of my own books was 'not proven', there was a note of censure attached to my file. Friends advised that I leave the BBC, now that I was undeniably a marked man. Surely, they said, the next time I'd be accused of taking a pencil or paperclip that allegedly did not belong to me. I rejected their advice, out of some sense of pride, of not wanting to surrender and to be pushed out, but mostly of not wanting to tell my mother that I had failed again, after medical school; that all of her sacrifices had been for nothing. I was forty-three and now had three children of my own. I stayed.

A few years later, the managers in my new department decided that all staff would be relocated to a new open-plan office. There was no more talk of slave plantations from me; the new breed of managers had got their way. A week or so before the big move, the seating plan was sent round in a group email to all of the members of the unit, including the fifteen or so colleagues with whom I shared a job description but not a skin colour.

Though I'd received the email, there was something weird about the seating plan. All of my colleagues were included in the plan but there was one name missing: mine.

I sent a jokey email to the planners saying, 'Is someone trying to tell me something?' My email went unanswered. When I wrote again, I received a terse response. There were not enough desks for everyone in the new office but a 'hot desk' would be available for me.

It had always been the case that temporary 'hot desks' were reserved for freelancers who came into the unit on a project-by-project basis. Nothing much had changed since the 1950s, when V.S. Naipaul wrote of the BBC's barely furnished freelancers' room on the second floor of the Langham Hotel, and the 'anxieties of the young or youngish men' who worked there, freelancers who would have given anything to be staff.

Being consigned to a freelancers' hot desk would not have mattered if I'd fitted Naipaul's description, but I was not young or a freelancer: I was mature, and had long been part of the staff.

I faced a dilemma about how to proceed. Since the last disciplinary hearing with the Man, I'd adopted a Buddhist attitude of avoiding conflict. Though slighted, I decided with some residual sense of shame not to pursue the matter; I let it slide.

A month after the move, I wandered into the open-plan space; and I felt as I had done when I first arrived at the Corporation twenty years ago, like a trespasser. I spotted a friendly face: J.B. We weren't close, but I'd always liked J.B. He was one of the more genial and erudite members of the department, with a wry sense of humour that verged on the subversive, but was ultimately consensual. Until recently, he'd been on attachment – on loan to another department – but had returned in time for the office move.

J.B. waved me over: 'I haven't seen you around for a while.'

'No, I don't have a desk.'

'You on attachment somewhere?'

'No,' I repeated, but without added emphasis, 'I don't have a desk.'

'You haven't left, have you?'

'No. Like I said, I'm desk-less. I was never assigned one.'

'Why not? What do you mean?'

'Well, look around you? What's different about me, would you say? And I'll give you a clue: it's not my height.'

J.B. looked perplexed. But gradually, his expression shifted to a kind of hurt, and then to affront and finally to outrage: 'That's rubbish. Being black has nothing to do with it!'

'Doesn't it?'

Within the space of a minute, no more, J.B. managed a

lengthy retort that included the words 'playing the race card' and 'chip on your shoulder' – the latter hadn't been levelled at me in twenty years. I suppose J.B. was as surprised and discomfited as I was to fall into such an unprecedented conversation. All along I had been mindful that we were in an open-plan office, so I'd barely raised my voice above a whisper. Even so, J.B. demanded to know why I was being 'so aggressive'!

Just a few hours previously, I'd walked past a billboard advertising a new book about race and identity, shouting about the uselessness of 'talking to white people about race', and I'd thought rather superiorly: a little simplistic, no? But now I found fellowship with the sentiment: there seemed little point in further discussion with J.B., who had begun to squirm. Eventually, trying to make light of the disagreement, he suggested I could have his desk on Fridays when he wasn't in. I declined, saying – in a way that I later felt was childish – 'I want my own bloody desk. I'm staff!'

It took a little while to regain my composure, but I did. 'What's going on here is a default to domain assumptions,' I said.

J.B. was intrigued. 'What do you mean by domain assumptions?'

'There are some who seem rightfully, unquestionably, to belong,' I stretched out my arm and gestured round the new office populated by white people. 'And then there are those who are other.'

J.B. was silent, and some part of me was sorry about that. But I regretted, too, that I'd exposed my racial anxiety. I'd revealed my own unsophistication and broken the unspoken pact that I'd made with all of my intelligent colleagues of J.B.'s sensibility, which was never to broach a subject as crude as race. I'd spent many years attending to the fragility of white colleagues like J.B., and he looked genuinely aggrieved and unsettled. No doubt, he'd grown accustomed to the idea that I, thankfully, wasn't like those other angry black folk. In our rarefied world of broadcasting, J.B. had never had to take recourse to saying, 'Oh, you're playing the race card' (which, in my experience, is actually the card white people play when they don't want to talk about race; shutting it down). Perhaps J.B. was disappointed with himself and with me for having forced from his lips such clichéd sentiments.

I was not even halfway through telling Uncle Castus what had happened when he started to laugh. He paused, apologised and laughed some more. When I finished my tale, I asked him what he thought.

'Well, Colin, I always told you, you were special!'

He broke in when I threatened to put the phone down. 'Don't be a pussy,' he said.

'What am I supposed to do now?'

'With your beautiful career?'

'Yes, where do I go from here?'

Castus told me to hold fire. He'd think on it and send me an email. I waited a couple of days. When no email arrived, I rang him again.

'I decided to put it in a letter,' he said. 'I thought it would have more kick.'

Earlier that morning the postman had been and there was still a spread of envelopes, some sticking out of the letterbox and others on the floor. 'Hold on,' I told him whilst I went to check and quickly picked up the envelope bearing Castus's distinctive cursive writing. I balanced the phone between my right ear and shoulder and opened the letter.

'It's from you.'

'Read it. Read it out loud,' he commanded. 'Don't scan it first. Just read it. Let me hear.'

'You're a right royal pain, you know that.'

'Just read the damn thing.'

'Are you sitting comfortably?' I asked, and then began to read.

My dear Colin,

You have received a setback, but it need not be lasting. Here are some instructions for surviving in and beyond the BBC: Remove gold from teeth and Afro-pick from hair. Actually, lose the 'fro, too.

Don't roll through the building as if there's some private soundtrack going on in your head. Stride. Look like you have somewhere to go and that you care about getting there on time.

Buy a T-shirt and print on both sides: 'I Am a Journalist'. This will avoid confusion when you decline to open doors for colleagues as they swing through reception.

On your weekend off, if you go into the empty office to try to get ahead, when the security guard arrives checking on reports of a suspicious-looking person, let him know, without rancour, that you haven't seen anyone.

At the office party, if colleagues approach you holding either end of a broomstick, don't baulk, just bend over backwards and slide under. Do not be satisfied with applause. Finish off with an acrobatic backflip. Watch Cuba Gooding Jnr's Oscar acceptance speech if unsure how.

Recognise your strengths. You need to specialise. You are one of the few people in the BBC who can say the word 'nigger'. It must be used in context. Do not say to your boss when you arrive for work in the morning, 'Yo, what's happening my nigga?'

When instructed to attend diversity initiative training, raise eyebrows along with everyone else. When the line manager turns to you, as the obvious expert on such matters, avoid rolling your eyes and break the awkward, extended silence with, 'it's political correctness gone mad!'

You may, now that you're nearing the end of your career, feel compelled to express a contrary opinion. Do not.

Now that you have survived your, what is it, fourth disciplinary hearing, do not be surprised when you find yourself invited to another. You are a very special category, reserved for the special ones. At the next hearing, as with this one, you will be encouraged to make a counter-claim against your detractors; you may feel redeemed and in the clear. You are not. At this stage, you will be accused of being tall and black. Deny it.

If, after your twentieth year, BBC managers canvas for volunteers for early redundancy, do not be surprised by how speedily your application will be accepted.

Replace gold in teeth; accept permanent loss of 'fro.

Yours,
Uncle Castus

I came to the end of the letter and released a long and loud sigh.

'What do you reckon?' Castus asked.

'I think it's the best thing you've ever written.'

'Really?'

'No! What the rass! You think this is some kind of joke?'

'What did I tell you?' All the humour had suddenly drained from Castus's voice. 'I told you not to join the bloody BBC. Didn't I tell you? This was always going to be the end game, you silly sod. You need to get out before they push you out. You're not special, just another nigger. And bwoi, it's later than you think.'

'Have you never stopped to think,' I asked, 'that I may be

sticking and staying to make it easier for the next black man to swing through those doors at the BBC? Maybe I'm black so *he* won't have to be!'

'That's just plain stupid,' answered Castus. 'There won't be another one after you. Not a real black man, anyway. You fulfil the strategy that they never have to encounter a real black man. You're like that grinning fool that allows them to say, "Well, how can you accuse me of being racist when one of my best friends is black?" You should pay greater attention to your "friend" Baldwin. You are the disagreeable mirror pretending that they, your liberal white friends and employer, are not what they are. Don't waste time reassuring white people that "they do not see what they see" – I'm quoting Mr Badass Baldwin here. It's utterly futile, since "they do see what they see: an appallingly oppressive and bloody history that they would rather not be reminded of." And yes, Colin, you do help them in that regard; you enable them.'

'Have you finished?'

'What, are you going to cry now?' asked my uncle. 'Go ahead and cry.'

Jazz, Maya, Toby

Walk good

I remained a few more years at the BBC. Even though it was unpleasant at times, I stuck and stayed. I did so in part because of my failure to complete the course at medicine and become a doctor, but mostly out of an old debt to my parents, Ethlyn and Bageye. In 1972, after sitting the entrance exam for St Columba's College, a private school in St Albans, Bageye had underscored his commitment to the unaffordable expense of my education by explaining to the curious headmaster that he didn't want his son to suffer the shameful experiences and lack of opportunities he'd endured as a child; he wanted something better for me. That same sentiment informed my determination to shield my own children from their grandfather. I'd never wanted to expose them to even a hint of the brutal and bruising encounters that had shaped my siblings' and my life under Bageye. I wanted it until I didn't want it.

'Pops has passed,' announced Milton on the other end of the phone. He'd rung, as had been expected, in the early hours of the morning with the news that Bageye had died.

'Pops? You mean Bageye?'

'Our father has died,' Milton repeated patiently. 'I'll ring again in a day or so with the funeral arrangements.'

I was still in bed and didn't exactly roll over and go back to sleep, but I did consider what it all meant without reaching a conclusion. Before I dropped off, though, I rang Milton back. My brother was an ex-RAF man but, in his approach to life and order, he'd never really left the military. He lived by a code of simple axioms: *prior planning prevents poor performance*; *tidy room, a tidy mind*. When his own time came, Milton's gravestone would probably bear the inscription: *He was always neat*.

I was in Morocco and was not due back for a few days. I asked Milton to ensure that all of Bageye's stuff was kept. I wanted to have a look through it. I didn't expect there to be anything of value, but I was sure my kids, especially, would be interested in any mementos. 'Mmmmh we'll see,' said Milton. 'There's no point keeping junk.'

Days later, Milton got in touch again to inform me that everything had been arranged for the funeral. Bageye was to be cremated. Milton had spoken to and appointed a priest – 'She's a woman, but she's actually all right' – and had the timings ready to give me. He, as the eldest son, would speak for five minutes. I could have two minutes. The priest would address the congregation for thirteen minutes. There'd be two songs, finishing with Frank Sinatra's 'My Way'.

'How does that all sound?' Milton asked. 'Awful,' I replied. 'Well, just remember,' he said, batting aside my complaint, 'you've got two minutes. Don't go over!'

I still found Milton's attitude baffling. Throughout our childhood when the demon entered Bageye and violence flashed through the house, Milton would bolt next door to take refuge at Mrs Robinson's until the shouting could no longer be heard through the adjoining wall. Somehow, my brother had recalibrated the past in a kind of dreamy dissolve that always marked those happy-ending, 1960s Hollywood transformations.

There were still a few relatives, including Selma, to be

informed about Bageye's demise and funeral, In recent years, the nearest I'd come to communicating with my eldest sister was the aborted phone call engineered by Richard, her former Saatchi & Saatchi colleague. I still had her number, so I rang Selma to tell her the news. 'Yeeeees?' she said, picking up the receiver with that familiar questioning voice of amusement and mischief. I spoke evenly and plainly as an underling might in a dispatch to his military commander. Selma paused before eventually answering in a way that Bageye would have done had he been told of an associate's death: 'If it so, then it so.' We both laughed, but my sister's tone cooled when I suggested that she might put her antipathy to one side and attend the funeral. Selma spoke quickly and hotly, explaining the impossibility of paying her respects to the old man as she'd be on an expensive photoshoot for Saatchi & Saatchi. Halfway through her monologue she stopped the pretence, caught up with herself, and spoke more calmly but with a steeliness that would brook no counterargument. My big sister reminded me that long ago she'd made a pledge never to spend any more time in Satan's (Bageye's) presence, dead or alive. 'Alive or dead,' she repeated.

I envied Milton's attitude, but couldn't quite bring myself to grieve for my father. Like Selma, I'd never stopped loathing him for his past cruelty and violence. But how do you behave when your tormentor is dead? How do you mark and register his importance? You probably don't reach for inspiration from Auden's 'Stop All the Clocks'. Grief was not a sentiment I recognised. My days at medical school might have skewed my feelings towards death; I don't think I'd ever reached a satisfactory approach.

My brother and father were both a curious mix of submerged emotions punctuated by bouts of hyper-sentimentality. Shuttling back in time, I now remembered an occasion in the early 1970s when walking past an old people's home in Luton with my father. He stopped, pulled me to one side and said with some urgency: 'Promise me you'll never let me end up in a place like dat.' I was probably ten; Bageye was in his forties. A sliver of a tear lined his eyelid. I thought it odd, on account of the fact that our father rarely confided in us. I didn't answer him. An out-of-place word to him might trigger an explosion; if he spoke, you did not necessarily speak back.

The reneged agreement on the old people's home was not mentioned when we'd met thirty years later in his sheltered accommodation. In any event, the home wasn't miserable; it was more holiday retreat than halfway house for the nearly dead.

Milton rang on the morning of the funeral with further instructions. When he repeated the address for the crematorium, I asked for the co-ordinates. He sighed: 'Don't be late!'

Of course, when we reached Luton (I drove with Ethlyn, Jo and the children), I managed, having resisted the calls to buy a satnav, to get us lost. Everyone had been directed by Milton to recce at the crematorium at 13:00 hours. We ended up not at the crematorium but at the funeral home.

The hearse hadn't left and, though I still felt antipathy towards Bageye, some sense of pity filled me at the sight of it, and at the thought that Bageye was all alone and had been neglected at this final stage. We were glad to have taken the wrong turn to the funeral home (at least that's how I characterised it), as we'd be the only car in the funeral cortège on the drive to the cemetery.

Ethlyn sat beside me in the passenger seat and kept up a monologue throughout the journey which seemed to be the expression of internal thoughts not meant for anyone's consumption but her own. It was repetitive and incantatory, the language had evolved in a lifetime's association with Christianity, most recently at the Calvary Church of God in Christ, and culminated in a wailing revelation, 'This is the final journey, the final journey, yes Lord!' Whatever was said, Ethlyn always came back to this end point.

I'd grown used to my mother's penchant for drama, but it was never a call for any intervention, and, in any case, it didn't ever seem wise to break her flow. Round and round she went, as if embarked on a never-ending cycle of prayers, in a resigned and reassuring voice, directed to that part of herself, the Cassandra part, that had always foreseen it would come to this: 'The final journey!' But when we stopped at a set of traffic lights Ethlyn was briefly thrown off her stride and out of her mantra. She looked up and peered ahead at the hearse bearing the coffin and said, 'Wait, is him in there?' It was uncanny how she suddenly broke from the trance, and then resumed when we reassured that Bageye was indeed in the coffin.

When our car eventually pulled into the cemetery's car park, such was the level of Milton's fulminating exasperation with me that when he began to speak the words made no sense. There was no real time for him to chastise his stupid, cavalier brother, and Milton had more urgently to address the concerns of some of Bageye's discontented spars.

For many of the West Indians shuffling in, the crematorium was itself a betrayal. There were noticeable rumblings, whispers and murmurs of doubt that Bageye's will would have contained instructions for a cremation. A West Indian had to be buried, surely? Another childhood memory surfaced: my father's angry mantra to his ungrateful children that one day we would 'bawl when dem screw down the coffin lid'. In the 70s, we had mocked the English for their battened-down emotions; for their dry, demure weddings and funerals. But here, now, as Milton gave his eulogy, there was hardly any bawling.

When it was my turn to speak, I stood and began by announcing that what I had to say couldn't be achieved in two minutes. Milton let out a loud 'Oh no.'

I'd decided to read from my book *Bageye at the Wheel* and chose what I thought was one of the funnier passages. Halfway through the reading there had been no laughter and, looking up and over the congregation, the thought that should have been obvious from the beginning occurred to me: wrong audience!

It was some consolation to learn soon after that I wasn't the only one to have misjudged the occasion. Thirteen minutes of unremitting awfulness began. Straining for profundity, the vicar's speech, as she pondered the whereabouts of the spirit of the man she called Clinton, would even have enraged Bageye with its banality. I imagined him forcing the lid of the coffin and scurrying to the bar or to Mrs Night's all-weekend poker game. A number of people talked all the way through the dirge. The cloying sentimentality of Frank Sinatra was a relief.

At the wake at The Chequers, Mrs Paulette, who'd started me on the journey to a reunion with Bageye when I'd rung the pub a few years back looking for him, had put up a poster with a photograph of Clinton George Grant, with 'AKA Bageye' helpfully spelt out underneath for the majority who knew him by no other name. The West Indian food and rum punch brought a flavour of the islands and the past. As we entered the pub, Ethlyn, who must have had a reserve tank of emotion (I thought she'd expended it all in the car as we'd followed the hearse), began to well up. 'This is the final journey,' she cried again. 'The last journey.' Perhaps the tears were not for Bageye but for herself; for the recognition of her own mortality and the understanding that, like Bageye and the last of that generation who still called themselves West Indian, England was likely to be her final resting place, too.

There were a dozen or so old-timers lined up at the bar who'd soon be following Bageye. Their presence in such numbers, though, was puzzling. I hardly recognised any of them from the crematorium, but they nodded meaningfully when our eyes met. Of course, they wouldn't have let something as *meaningless* as a funeral interrupt them placing a bet on the 2:30 at Newmarket, and neither would Bageye, I suppose. But what were they doing at The Chequers, I asked Milton. 'Stop your noise,' was all I could get out of my brother. 'Wind in your neck.'

I whispered the same question to Ethlyn. A smile rounded her lips. It gave her a chance to step out of the reverent character she'd assigned for the day. Her voice was high with the amused sarcasm that I loved to hear, as she explained that West Indians surely weren't going to miss out on free curry goat and Guinness on tap to wash it down. 'You mad!' Each man would eat and drink, belch and fart until 'dem belly full and dem batty glad'. My mother was right. They were having a merry old-time talk. And if I'd have looked at them askance, they'd have kissed their teeth and asked: 'What wrong with you? Cho, man you tek life too serious.'

Perhaps if I hadn't left home, gone to university and mixed predominantly with middle-class white people, I'd have felt more at home in their company; I was alien to these elderly West Indians and they to me, but Milton was fast on his way to becoming them, settling into a kind of performance of West Indianness. I had unwisely surrendered responsibility for the funeral arrangements to my brother and he'd carried them out with military precision. I reminded Milton that I'd asked him to set aside any of Bageye's personal things for me to look over before he discarded them. I asked my brother now, as we stepped outside, if we could go and check them out. 'Wait here,' he said and walked off up the street.

When Milton returned he handed me a Morrisons carrier bag.

'What's this?'

'Take a look.'

'No, what is this? What's the meaning of this?'

'Well,' said Milton, as if speaking to a bright, but temperamental child, 'they're our father's personal effects.'

'Where's the rest of it?'

'The rest was junk.'

Inside the plastic bag were half a dozen photos, several empty picture frames, and a battery-operated wall clock.

'The *rest* was junk?'

'I knew you'd be like this,' said Milton, turning on his heels and walking away. 'I'm going to see how Mother's doing.'

As my brother entered the pub, Jo and the kids exited from the same door. They nodded at each other as people do a thousand times on such occasions. They came and stood beside me. The day's proceedings suddenly seemed to have caught up with us. There was a sad silence; none of us spoke.

I held the plastic bag and wondered about what was missing – Bageye's rings, the heavy watch and his array of hats. A repetitive sound was coming from within the bag. It was the plastic clock, still ticking. I considered taking out the battery. That was the right thing to do, wasn't it? I hesitated and Jo, sensing my dilemma, gently took the plastic bag from me. She opened it, found the clock and removed the battery; the clock stopped.

'You will remember this day.'

Jazz, our thirteen-year-old daughter, woke her younger siblings, Maya and Toby with this incantation.

I'd said the phrase so often that it had become a family joke and mantra; they'd teased me, repeating, 'You will remember this day,' whenever I'd suggested that a treat was in store. Yet this was going to be an extraordinary day. For today, after such a long time, skirting around the subject of Bageye, shielding them from him, we were taking the children to see their grandfather, for the very first time.

A mystique had taken hold in their minds about this much-mythologised man. I'd been responsible inadvertently for that. They'd been clamouring for quite a while to meet him, probably ever since I first mentioned his peculiar name; now my resistance had broken.

Once, a few months after my troubled reunion with Bageye, driving down the motorway from Yorkshire back home to Brighton, I'd suggested that maybe we could swing by and see the old man. But, as one, alarmed by the prospect and unprepared for its suddenness, they'd all objected. 'You can't just drop that bomb on us,' Jazz protested. I'd conceded that it was a rash idea and accelerated at the sign for Junction 11, speeding past the turning as Luton approached.

Now, though, it was happening, really, really happening. At breakfast, the children seemed more sullen and apprehensive than excited. When I'd spoken of my father in the past, I'd conjured a bogeyman. Was it so surprising then that they'd be trepidatious now? I asked them, in turn, what image of Bageye came to mind when they thought of him.

Maya considered him 'pervy' as Bageye went with prostitutes (I'd previously recounted how my mother would berate her husband when leaving the house for gambling and partying to 'gwan, run to your blue foot'). Jazz pictured him as a 'tyrannical wife- and child-beating monster', and Toby, the youngest, was just nervous of the thought of him, although in some ways, he didn't really believe that Bageye existed; he was just a story.

All along the motorway, we continued the conversation; the kids peppering me with questions about Bageye, beyond the rudimentary offerings I'd made over the years, as if cramming at the last minute, in preparation for an imminent exam. The fact that there were no photos of Bageye made him seem even scarier to them. I mean, dear God, if this man was not so terrifying then why would every single photo of him have been excised from all of the family albums? There were no portraits of Bageye but neither were there any of his family. Throughout my childhood, I don't recall one event when he spoke of his father, and it was possible to make the case that I had continued the tradition of silence. Apart from a few repeated snippets, I had never discussed my father with Jazz, Maya or Toby.

We exited the motorway and edged towards the town centre. All of my brothers and sisters had moved on from Luton, one by one, and eventually Ethlyn had left, too. Now only Bageye remained. I'd never considered Luton to be grim before, but from the sounds coming from the back seats, I judged the children considered it to be so. They peered out of the window, not out of a sense of wonder it seemed; from the rear-view mirror, I was embarrassed to see their expressions of bewilderment, and turned quickly back – eyes on the road – before my gaze caught theirs. Toby wanted to know whether only tiny people lived in the 'teeny-weeny' terraced houses. Jazz voiced a sad disbelief: 'This is where you lived? This is where *he* lives?'

'It's not all that bad,' I said.

Some kind of force field prevented Maya from initially crossing the threshold into the assisted living building that housed her grandfather. She'd always been an outlier, sensitive to emergent auras and bad vibes, and we were all sensitised to her sensitivity. Her hesitancy underlined the awkwardness that perhaps we all felt, but were unable to express. Wisely, Jazz held open the dodgy swing door and eventually Maya rushed through the opening as if hurrying out of a heavy rain that had just begun to fall.

Bageye was at his front door on the third floor waiting as we climbed the staircase. I was struck once again by how tiny he seemed; my father was barely taller than Jazz. He immediately focused on Toby's afro. 'Barbers have to work as well you know, my friend,' he laughed. Toby laughed as well, and there was a bit of a chain reaction. My father was obviously grateful. This time, it felt as if I was his sponsor and Bageye was auditioning for the part of dutiful grandfather. I fell into willing him silently, as we sat down, to succeed, to show his hidden bona fides and talent that surely existed. If he'd had a set of false teeth, I'd have encouraged him to do something funny with them, pull them out or pretend to swallow them. Then tap dance perhaps, or stand on his head. Anything. Something. Not nothing. But having made a good start at putting at least Toby at ease, he struggled to follow through.

'Me don't have no cards in the house,' Bageye said when I suggested he show the kids his expertise in shuffling. He might well have added that he had no ganja growing on the windowsill, or loaded weapons in the drawer. He appeared flummoxed, more so when he instantly mixed up Maya and Jazz as soon as they'd answered his question about their names.

'By the way, it's not My-yah,' said Maya. 'It's May-yah.'

'My-yah?'

'No. May . . .' She paused to allow Bageye to follow.

'May?'

'Yah.'

'Yah?'

'Now put the two together.'

'May-yah. You is good. A good teacher, you have here. She can go far. Remind me of . . .'

'Selma?' I answered.

'How you know!'

But nothing followed after that light-hearted exchange, save an unexpected silence. It was unclear now whose turn it was to speak or what to say. Bageye looked towards me as an actor might at the stage director in the prompt corner, signalling help for the next line.

'Perhaps a drink for the children?' I suggested.

'Yes, man. Some Coca-Cola in the fridge.'

I made my way to the kitchen, grabbed the over-sized bottle of Coca-Cola, liberated the few cups and glasses in the cupboard that weren't yet home to fossilised insects, and poured the smallest amounts into them.

'How are you getting on with the book?' I asked, taking a sip of my Coca-Cola.

'It don't finish,' he answered. I was not convinced that my father was ironically referring back to *Middlemarch* from our first conversation almost a year ago.

He made a spirited attempt at reaching out to Jo, mistaking her look for an Italian, notwithstanding her soft South Yorkshire accent. The children sat in a row glued to the settee, their eyes occasionally drawn to the sight of racehorses parading across the TV screen. They were more intrigued by the half-full jar of £2 coins and whispered among each other trying to guess the number of coins. I prayed for Bageye to open the jar and distribute the coins evenly to all three. He did no such thing; that treasure was reserved for his newly promoted favourite son, Milton, and *his* daughter.

Bageye scrambled for something, anything, to say. He went

through the inventory of his children asking me for an update on each. He paused when arriving at Christopher, lowering his voice.

'I hear him have some head trouble.'

'What? No. Who told you that?'

'Is just what I hear. Some trouble with the head.'

'No, he has epilepsy.'

'So, it true what them say?'

I gave up on hiding my irritation and refused to engage any more in the so-called conversation.

'Him change up?' Bageye's voice was tremulous and fearful. I realised that I'd never had a serious talk with my father. All the time, as a child, I'd listened in fearful awe as he spoke with other adults, marvelled at the simple truth and certainty of his opinions. Even with my mother's characterisation 'If you want jackass for ride, here comes Bageye,' it had never occurred to me that he might be foolish, ignorant and bigoted. I'd not had the chance in the intervening thirty-two lost years to see and interrogate the contours and limits of his mind. And I realised that, at this moment, I preferred him to remain the old, familiar, evil wretch.

'The head trouble him?'

'Why don't you ask him yourself,' I said, taking out my phone and dialling Chris's number. But Bageye refused to take the mobile from me when I held it out. Chris answered and I apologised, saying it was a bum call, before putting the phone back in my pocket.

'That was nasty,' said Bageye. 'You didn't have to do that. Rough me so. I don't especially dig that. Embarrass me in front of the pickney.'

'Sorry,' I said, brushing aside his complaint. 'Shall we think about some food for the children?'

Bageye gave the impression it was a trick question. 'What time you have?' He asked. When told, he went on to say that if we hurried we could catch Mrs Paulette for some lunch at The Chequers.

We rounded up the children. Bageye chose his hat – a fedora – for the day.

'OG,' I said, and the kids laughed.

'OG? A wha' that?' Bageye asked.

'OG, with the hat. You know 'original gangster' like George Raft or James Cagney, with the fedora. You know, the original gangster.'

'Me you a-call gangster? I am not a gangster.'

'It was a joke.'

'Plenty man make joke like that a-end up in a cold grave.'

Bageye struggled to get into his jacket and out of his mood made vex by my bad remark and worse still by the sight of the glasses of Coca-Cola that not one of the children had touched. 'That drink cyann drink again, you know sport,' he said to me. 'Cho. Spoil now, cyann drink again.' He'd just about shaken off the remnants of the mounting aggravations by the time we reached the chair lift. He suggested he race the children down to the bottom. Toby rushed to beat him. Maya and Jazz, though, took their sweet time.

The pub was only a few minutes from the flat but, when we reached there and Bageye pushed ahead to place the order, he was met by Mrs Paulette who hardly spoke and mostly shook her head. The kitchen was closed, Bageye informed us. 'Paulette not bad-minded just sometime-ish,' he explained. 'You know how some woman stay.'

He suggested we head to the food market at the Arndale Centre where another West Indian, Mrs Henry, ran a cafe.

'Isn't she sometime-ish, too?' I asked.

'Sometime,' Bageye replied drily.

We filed along to the Arndale Centre, once sparkling and modernist, now slightly dishevelled, low-rent and down at heel, just a stone's throw away from the pub. Luton, I hadn't appreciated as a child, was tiny. Everywhere was just five minutes away. Mrs Henry, who as well as running the premier West Indian cafe also had a food stall, was Mrs Paulette in twenty years' time, wind-dried and saltier. The first thing to get out of the way was some business over some yam, which my father had sent someone to buy from Mrs Henry on his behalf.

'Say I come and ask for a pound of yam and pick up dis?' Bageye reached for some yam, which was rotten at one end. 'What you gwan say to me?'

'First of all,' answered Mrs Henry, 'you don't have no business pick up the t'ing. You point and I pick it, give you.'

A simple purchase was not just a transaction, but an opportunity to discuss business models and home-spun philosophy.

'But the t'ing rotten; half of it no good.'

'Is so me buy it,' answered Mrs Henry, 'then so it must sell.'

It seemed a fierce argument but both were chuckling away and agreed at the end that it was best that Bageye did not send an inexperienced yam buyer in the future; they, she and Bageye, would talk it through and sort something out from here on in. It was 'black people time' after all, and black people 'mus' treat one another good!'

Bageye introduced his special guests and Mrs Henry, looking down from the stall, wondered aloud how, as my father 'face favour bull' him have 'grand-pickney turn out pretty, pretty. Lord a-mercy!'

'Aye sah,' said Bageye.

He could not have been more pleased by the impression we were having on Mrs Henry and others who came to inspect us – applauding our three generations of family and faux friendliness: 'Is so family must stay, stay together, walk good' – and the consequent rise in his own stock.

The tetchiness between us, though, was never far from the surface. Perhaps it was truer to describe the nature of our relationship not as rapprochement but more as detente. Old wounds flared at the slightest knock. Bageye shot me the most vicious look and moved in front of me blocking my path to Mrs Henry when I had the temerity to get my wallet out in order to pay her up front, as was required, for everyone's meal. Bageye paid! Right is right, even though his stomach troubled him too much to join us.

As we tucked into the curry goat and rice, to be washed down with coconut water (my father had pointedly asked Mrs Henry to bring us anything other than Coca-Cola), Bageye wandered around the other stalls making small talk with old West Indian friends. He returned to the cafe, as we finished our meals, carrying a small plastic bag, but made no mention of it.

On the walk back to his home, Bageye pointed out the few buildings that marked the terrain of the physical and psychological map of his life. As well as Mrs Henry's West Indian cafe, there was The Chequers; a nearby Baptist church where he claimed to be a congregationalist and, finally, his two offices, Coral's and Ladbrokes' bookmakers. That was it. 'What more you need?' He asked.

When we reached the car park of the sheltered accommodation, he took out from the bag a newly purchased Afro-comb. Still in its plastic sheath, it had metal teeth and a wooden handle with Black Power fists emblazoned on them. 'I want you to have this,' he said, handing the comb to Toby, 'before the hair run riot and you have fi shave it clean off and start again.'

Toby beamed, but he was also embarrassed. There was only

one plastic bag and no other presents for Maya or Jazz. But they each enthused, inspecting the comb, as if it was some kind of talisman. Eventually, the comb was passed to Jo and she secured and fashioned it decoratively in Toby's hair. All that remained was to say goodbye; the traffic had built up as rush hour began so we moved inside, through the communal area to the staircase.

'Maybe next time you'll come to Brighton,' I said, for want of a better, or any, exit line.

'Yes, me soon come,' answered Bageye, without much conviction. He reminded Toby to not just admire the Afro comb but to use it. There was no suggestion from him or any of us really for some kind of goodbye embrace. Jo drew a line on any further awkwardness by gathering the children to her and repeating that the invitation to visit us in Brighton was something we'd all welcome.

'Yes, yes, God spare life, me soon come,' said Bageye, and again once more for emphasis, 'Me. Soon. Come.'

He positioned himself in the seat of the chairlift and snapped the protective flaps into position. My father was now secure in his chariot. We all waved farewell as Bageye, raising his fedora, ascended his own particular stairway, whether to heaven or hell I couldn't say, but it was clear that we wouldn't see him or his like ever again.

'Without a vision,' the Bible says, 'the people perish.' I know this because my mother told me so. It was always Ethlyn, not Bageye, who was the source – of everything. Like so many, my father, in the novelist and poet George Lamming's memorable phrase, 'had only fathered the idea of me [and] left me the sole liability of my mother who really fathered me'.

A mother's prayer for her children is a kind of silent

activism, willing them into righteousness – for what they are, they should be. But what was this vision? As far as Ethlyn was concerned, it was to stretch up and up onto your tiptoes as high as you could go, and reach for that which was tantalisingly just beyond reach. Ethlyn did this, even when her body convulsed, when her memories told her otherwise, when she reached beyond her capacity to forgive Bageye his many transgressions, to accompany him on his final journey, just ahead of her own.

A decade after the kids had first met Bageye (who would die months later), Jo and I invited them back home to lunch, to reflect on the drama and meaning of that encounter, to consider how Bageye, alongside Ethlyn, in shaping my attitude towards fatherhood and Caribbeanness, might have moulded theirs, too. All three were young adults now, and had surprised me by embracing a growing feeling for their Caribbean heritage. In their childhood, I had only offered them a dialled-down version, to make room for the fact, desired or not, of their and my Englishness. I had paid attention to Uncle Castus's assertion, 'I'm black so you don't have to be,' and applied it to my upbringing of them as well. With the passage of time, whether at school, university or the BBC, I had expected to become more and more invisible or, at least, for my colour not to be so dominant. That was the dream, right? To be able to disappear into British society and go about your business unmolested? In reality, especially in the last decade, the culture had forced me in the other direction: I had become blacker. I was fascinated to hear that Toby, Maya and Jazz felt the same.

'I thought I'd become Jamaican once I met Bageye,' said Maya. Jazz and Toby agreed. Toby recalled observing his grandfather chatting to the Caribbean people in the Arndale Centre and 'thinking that was kind of cool'.

We had sat and eaten curry goat in the high-ceilinged market hall and Jazz and Maya had both been struck by the pity of it, the sadness that an aspect of Caribbean culture, unknown to them, had been within touching distance all along: 'There was a Jamaican influence there,' said Maya. 'I didn't realise that. Not like Brighton. And that Jamaican food stall . . . that was the first time I'd ever seen that.'

We were all a little shy of the subject and eased into it. I had hoped that I'd been able to shield them from the trauma of my childhood by not focusing on it, fudging or changing the subject when raised, but it was clear that there had been leakage; there was a kind of generational trauma they had been affected by in my presence as they grew up with me and Jo.

Toby confessed: 'I'm nervous now imagining being that kid and that we're going to see him again. I knew he was a villain.'

As our children spoke about the villain, I found myself peculiarly feeling defensive of Bageye, arguing that he'd have been nervous about meeting all of us as a block, possibly already schooled in thinking unkindly of him. 'I'd have been wary if I was him; it wasn't easy. It must have been uncomfortable for him. Suddenly all these aliens had arrived.' I sought vainly to protect Bageye, but the sleights kept coming in thick and fast:

'So he just didn't like his own children?'

'He couldn't deal with his own children.'

'Yeah, he constantly needed to be doing better for the children and was constantly thwarted, we'll give him that.'

'He must have always been letting, what, at least seven young people down.'

'He wasn't providing! That must have been an embarrassing thought.'

On and on went Maya, Jazz and Toby without let-up, or

allowance for any intervention from me, before returning to what they perceived to have been Bageye's coldness or, at best, coolness:

'He wasn't very friendly. He didn't even give us a hug.'

'I was hoping he'd immediately have some sort of connection. Not that I liked the idea of him, but I hoped for some sort of ignited feeling of some kind of compassion or even him just remembering my name would have been a start.'

'I thought he was going to be this spicy Jamaican guy who was up for having us in his life from now on.'

'Not a chance.'

'I looked around the flat thinking of our inheritance, but I don't think he even had anything worth stealing.'

'I was glad it was over, whoof.'

'Didn't you think we'd ever see him again?'

'Nah, next time it would be in his coffin.'

'Enough!' I said reflexively.

Jazz, Maya and Toby eventually saw something in me that caused them to pause. I'd invited it on myself, this unmitigated torrent of feeling which poured forth from them, until finally, I'd felt like a corner man whose failing and battered pugilist, Bageye, was taking too awful a pummelling in the ring and had no choice other than to throw in his towel. One by one Maya, Jazz and Toby pushed back out of their chairs, stood and made their way to me and placed their hands on my shoulders.

I realised that for as long as I could remember, I had been apologising to myself – for my father. No matter which way you cut it, Bageye was a disappointment, but he was also the product of an upbringing not marked by tenderness in a colony, an outpost of empire still scarred and embarrassed by the legacy of slavery.

Throughout their childhood, I had only drawn our kids' attention selectively to the great calamity that has been perpetrated on black people over many generations; I didn't want to expose them to that history, to have them take into their souls the idea that ours was a story of victimhood. We were the descendants of the enslaved who, even as they'd fought back, rebelled and brought about their own emancipation, had been brutalised, branded, mentally and physically violated, killed and disposed of.

Once, when they were still youngsters, Jo and I took Jazz, Maya and Toby to visit the International Slavery Museum in Liverpool. But outside of the museum, we all picked up on each others' hesitation. No one wanted to enter the ghoulish chamber, as I saw it, of torture and shame. Jo and I let them know that they didn't have to go in; she led them away in search of a happier experience. I went into the museum alone – for them; an act which was a kind of sacrifice, I suppose, a version of what Castus had always said: he was black so I didn't have to be. It was a myth really. Though there was no way round blackness, in Liverpool that afternoon, such a notion could be deferred.

But there comes a time in this country when every parent of black children feels compelled to give them 'the talk' about the various perils in store for them that threaten the black body, adrift in a liminal space many characterise as Babylon. The 'talk' is in recognition that the British State is waiting to pounce on you; it has mapped out a plan and a path that will demonise and criminalise you, propelling you along the pipeline that channels too many black youths from school through expulsion and on to prison. Bageye's version of 'the talk' was accompanied with a belt and the warning: 'If you cyann hear, then you will feel.' He may have failed in other areas of parenthood but, like many of his West Indian spars who were also fathers, he had one area of expertise: he was a world-class beater. I imagine Bageye thought he was doing us a favour. The logic was simple: we were under surveillance in Britain. If his pickney didn't absorb the lessons of the proportionate 'licks' meted out by him, then we were liable to suffer the malicious consequences of a far more punitive State.

A life of watchfulness, of living on amber alert, can be wearing. Reflecting back on it, the deficits are many, and I did not want my children to be battle-hardened by Britain. I did not want them to live with the expectation of humiliation that many of the black families whose households I entered in the 1960s and 70s accepted as a given. I had always been perplexed by how the larger-than-life West Indian adults I knew back then seemed to shrink somewhat in the company of white people. It was pitiable and disappointing. Often it felt, growing up, that black fathers especially were embarrassed that they could do little more than prepare their children for a lifetime of expected degradations. Bageye, though he spoke little of it, would have shrugged and said, 'The world is as it is . . . mek your peace with it.'

Ethlyn, like so many West Indian mothers who were petrified for their children, counselled that we should avoid conflict. The same sober advice has not been necessary for my children. They might pang for the missed Caribbean connections when growing up in the absence of people of colour in Brighton. They may have been late to the party, but are making up for it now. There's a Caribbean exuberance, sense of mischief and search for rapture in all of them that is heartening to see; I feel more Caribbean in their presence. And though they recognise the disadvantages that British society imposes on blackness, they do not expect to be stymied by it.

Increasingly, I see that they, and their generation, are recasting what it is to be British, and what it is to be descended from the likes of Ethlyn and Bageye.

My father was a man of many hats. The choice of hat signified his mood – the trilby meant a win at the horses or poker game, the Russian Cossack-like hat signalled that he was setting out for a business deal (most likely involving marijuana), the flat corduroy cap suggested defeat, an overdue bill that couldn't be paid, a catastrophic gambling loss. As a child, I lived in awe and fear of Bageye's choice of hat.

Recounting that assessment to my children, they understood that the hats also signified Caribbean elan, individualness – a kind of local bella figura. On one of my birthdays a dozen or so years ago, I was emotionally caught off guard when Jazz, Maya and Toby presented me with a huge wrapped present. I tore through the wrapping paper. Inside was a bundle of straw and cloth hats. I could not contain my tears. They bid me put on one of the hats and, as one, all nodded approvingly: 'Style! Yes man. Fresh.'

Acknowledgements

Editor
Bea Hemming

Agent
Sophie Lambert

The Family
Ethlyn
Bageye
Sedonie
Stephen
Sonia
Clint
Lurane
Chris
Robert
Viv
Jo
Jazz
Maya
Toby

Advisers
Jo Alderson
Nick Rankin
Sharmilla Beezmohun

Emma Dyer
Edson Burton

Researcher
Sonia Grant

Cover Art
Jazz Grant

Cover Design
Matthew Broughton
Yeti Lambregts

Author photo
Miss Ohio

Copy-editor
Vimbai Shire

Proofreader
Fiona Brown

Editorial Manager
Graeme Hall

Publicist
Anna Redman Aylward

Marketer
Kate Neilan

Production Controllers
Shabana Cho
Polly Dorner